TO: Michael

Thank you

Do it with Fire !

ONE YOU, ONE ME

Matty Guariglia

PROMINENCE PUBLISHING

Editing assistance by Brian Ruffino.

Prominence Publishing
www.prominencepublishing.com

The author can be reached as follows:
www.mattyguariglia.com or mguariglia@yahoo.com.

Cover photography by Thomas Hicklin www.hicklinphotography.com

One You, One Me/ Matty Guariglia. -- 1st ed.

ISBN: 978-1-988925-32-5

Contents

Introduction

I have been studying self-improvement for over ten years. All the experiences I went through have given me a doctorate degree in how to overcome adversity and push through the grit. Throughout this process, I learned how to have a positive outlook, a driven mindset and, above all else, a bulletproof mentality. I've learned how to bounce back, withstand the pain, get out of debt, start businesses, keep it moving and fight for what's mine. Throughout this book, I will teach my philosophy and mindset on how to endure things that come up against you and how to overcome various roadblocks. You have to have a fire that burns deep. For a year straight, I took cold showers and had no heat; I ate ramen noodles and bologna. I had bologna coming out my ears. My personal relationship with GOD was my foundation, my rock. When you're down and out you have to make a decision, keep fighting or give in. I refuse to give in. If I fall, I get back up and keep moving forward. Don't let anyone discourage you, keep a distance from the negative and weak-minded people. Be strong and don't give up. Once we take responsibility and stop feeling sorry for ourselves, we begin to climb the hill of self-mastery. We can achieve whatever we set out to do. Dream it, have faith it's going to happen, then put it into action.

I believe this book can help anyone and everyone: entrepreneurs, business owners, teachers, labors, cashiers, any career, students, hustlers, grinders, people in massive debt, the rich and the wealthy... I'm telling you what I been through and how I switched my thinking. I came from a very humble beginning and became successful through hard work and the grace of GOD. The struggle doesn't care about your background; it will eat you up and spit you out. It comes down to a mindset, and if you don't keep a positive outlook on things, you won't be in the right state of mind. In the last couple of years, more and more people have come to me for advice, so that is the main reason why I was inspired to write this book.

I enjoy helping people. I get a high when I help someone elevate and get better. There's no other feeling like it. If I can inspire someone to get off the couch and get things done, I would be extremely grateful. I believe when people read this book, they will get real value and gain some insight on my personal philosophies and beliefs that could help them. I'm far from perfect; I don't claim to have some magic answer, the real answer to life is inside us. We have to find ourselves within. It may sound cliché to some, but it's the absolute truth, and once you humble yourself and understand the truth in that statement, I believe you can achieve great works in your life. Things such as relationships, jobs, businesses, writing or whatever it is in your inner you that makes you move. In this book, you'll find ways to help you get there, and hopefully, I make you think about certain things, as you reach inside and pull out greatness. One thing I can tell you is to have fire (Fuego) and a lion's attitude. You need to believe in yourself. Have faith that you can do anything and don't let people talk you out of your dreams. Haters can hate while you count your stacks at the bank.

Never say can't. In junior high my teacher Mr. Maxwell had our whole class go outside and write the word "can't" on a piece of paper and bury it in the ground. A few weeks ago, I had my family do the same thing. We went to the backyard, and I had them all write the word "can't" on a piece of paper, and we buried it. It had a psychological effect on my way of thinking. So I hope to have the same effect on my kids. And hopefully, everyone who reads this does it with their kids, family, and friends. Write the word "can't" on paper then have your kids, family, friends, or yourself put it in the ground and bury it. Say I will not, or we will not ever use this weak word again. We can do anything. We always have to be prepared because people don't want to see you shine. So be ready for everything at all times, don't let your guard down. We must learn, all of us including myself, to brush off the hate and keep it moving. Don't give people the satisfaction of taking you under. Smile and wave at those hating!

I was walking with a property manager who managed 278 units and said to him, "I'm going to own this one day." He laughed and thought I was joking, but I was dead serious. I 100% believe I will own hundreds, probably thousands, of units and investment properties in the near future. It doesn't matter what people think about our dreams. Most of the time when your goals are extraordinary most people won't understand, and that's ok. You do what you got to do and keep moving forward.

Life is a journey; just be yourself and enjoy the ride. Our potential is infinite; we can achieve so much greatness, it's up to us as individuals to advance as far we want to take it. I love how Muhammad Ali referred to himself as the greatest! He said it, believed it and was. You have to believe in yourself.

One You, One Me

One of the most interesting facts of life is that there is only one of you and only one of me. Embrace your individuality. No matter how much someone tries to be like you, they will never do it the way you do it. That's why we should enjoy being ourselves. We're all unique in our own way. Embrace who you are and love yourself. I'm not saying to be conceited. What I'm saying is treat yourself well and don't beat yourself up. We're all special, and we all have gifts, we just have to find it and activate what we're good at. We're probably all self-conscious about something which is ok, but in reality, you should try and get over things. It would be nice if I were taller... I'm 5'8", but I feel 6'2" ha-ha. I am what I am and feel blessed just to be alive. Accepting who we are is important. The cool thing about ourselves is we get to choose what type of person we become. We have a decision to make on how we live our life.

We can be kind to others and help people, or not. We have thousands of choices daily on how we choose to live. Being yourself is fun because in reality there are no rules. We become chiseled and have defiant moments in our life when we overcome adversity and do the impossible. Usually, when we come up against great opposition and roadblocks, we are in arm's length of great success. Don't stop pursuing greatness just because there are some setbacks; you're too close – don't stop pushing. All the pain and sacrifice builds your character and shows the inner you, what you're made of.

How do you look at yourself? How do you carry yourself? What type of values do you have? These are some questions you should be asking yourself. Don't worry so much about how other people see you, look into yourself, how do you see yourself? If you have to make some changes that's fine, get started, do what is going to make you happy with yourself. You are what you think about, so try and keep your mind on good things. Don't settle for less. It's important to laugh, smile and have some fun. Do what makes you happy.

I feel all the craziness that happens along the way, all the broken bones, broken hearts, smiles, laughter, and all that good stuff is what defines us in this whirlwind of life that I love so much. I have found out things about myself that I had no clue I possessed. I endured a lot of pain, hardships, and heartaches. I also experienced unconditional love, great acts of kindness and so much joy. Finding yourself is a lifetime of experiences. I believe there is always room for growth, and if we believe we achieved the pinnacle, then we haven't learned much at all. Even though we're always trying to grow, it's good to get knocked on your butt from time to time because it strengthens us.

When we find ourselves it's different for everyone at different points in our life. It may be one defining moment, or it may be several instances that collectively define you. It's a sense of comfort and relaxation. The fact is that none of us are going to make it out alive. Sometimes I have to tell myself to relax; I can be wound up at times going 100 miles an hour. That's just me though. We all learn how to talk ourselves through things, and hopefully, we can be our self. It's a fun journey. As you get older you think back and say what a ride so far, I can't wait to see what's next. If you're young that's great news, enjoy the process, enjoy the journey and have fun! Soak up the sun. Soak up the waves, eat some good food, meet some cool people and don't forget to laugh. If you're young you should try and listen to your elders; sometimes we think we know more then we actually do. When I was younger, I always had a good ear to listen to someone who had already gone through it. Then there were times I listened but didn't pay much attention, then later down the road, it made a lot of sense. Just have an open mind. If you're older and there's still things you want to do or places you want to travel, I say go for it. You'll be glad you did.

You'll meet some good people and some shady people; people will make you happy, mad and everything else. Through these experiences we find ourselves, and we discover what we are made of. Always remember to be yourself, and when you truly find yourself, it will be natural. Finding your true self takes time and experience. Good luck out there! Although, I believe we make our own luck.

The older I get, the more I have been able just to be me. We all have different outlooks on life. What's important though, is we don't shy away from our true colors. And what I mean by that is our natural born fabric that makes up our being. If you like country music, be proud of it. Don't say you don't like it because your friend doesn't like it. If your favorite food is octopus tentacles, then be loud and proud. If you still bump Vanilla Ice and New Kids on the Block, it's ok. For the younger people reading this go YouTube it haha. Life is good! Enjoy being you. Try not to alter your way of living to make everyone else happy.

Most artists, musicians, actors, actresses, athletes, etc., copy or emulate the great ones before they eventually come into their own light. There are some motivational speakers that have charm and a flow pattern; some speakers are in your face and loud. Both methods are effective, just different styles. There are unlimited ways to get your point across. I work on myself every day, and it's a never-ending project. I know I'll be progressing and learning and working on myself for the rest of my days. I think too many of us worry about opinions. The people who are handing out negative opinions are usually the weak-minded people. They're usually the ones that are scared to try anything themselves, so they try and discourage you.

My ladies, when you're shining, good spirit, glow on your face, beautiful smile, nails done, hair looking fine, dress looking fly, shoes on point, there's going to be heads turning, haters spewing, people talking, and mad how you're walking. Good, Good and more Good! Let them hate while you be great! When you're doing well, it's good because you can start to weed out the fakes and phonies. Watch everyone's body language, breathing patterns, eye twitches, mouth mannerisms, hand and feet movements, the tone in their voice, all that and more. Be receptive to people, watch their reactions and movements when you're doing big things.

Now listen! I highly recommend moving in silence and keep your plans under wrap. The more people you tell, the more susceptible you are to get knocked off track. Someone could steal your idea or business. Someone may discourage you or talk you out of something that could have been successful. It's ok to talk to business partners, your lawyer, husband or wife and a close few who you can trust. Keep it very limited. I just dropped some serious GEMS, so I hope you paid attention and wrote down some notes. When I spot someone who I can tell is uncomfortable with my shine, I don't put them on blast; I know what to do and say around them. Then there are some people I have to cut off completely. It may sound harsh to some, but who wants haters or yes men around them all day. It's said that the five people you're around most reflect on you, so be careful who you hang with.

> *"Be uncommon amongst uncommon people"*
> *–David Goggins*

Bob Marley sang the words, "Don't worry about a thing, cause every little thing is gonna be alright." Life is good my people, enjoy it. I want you to read this part and repeat it daily. Or write your own. Say it every morning before you walk out the door. Look at yourself in the mirror and say it. You may think it's weird but so what? Try it for 30 days. If it does not affect you, then don't do it anymore. If you start to believe it, it will become a reality. You can have anything in life; you just have to confess it, believe it, and put action behind it.

Say it with me:

"I speak greatness,
I feel healthy,
love is in me,
I'm at peace,
I can do anything,
I'm ready,
I'm grateful,
success runs through my blood,
chains are broken,
thresholds against me are broken off,
everything around me is good,
my relationships are good,
my business is good,
my place of work is good,
I'm going to be alright,
I fear nothing but GOD,
the sun will shine,
I hustle, I grind, I shine,
I'm an amazing individual with integrity, loyalty, inspiration,
I'm a King, I'm a Queen,
I will not be defeated, broke down or beaten,
I am strength, I am strong,
I will push through, breakthrough,
I have a fire inside me that burns deep,
I'm hungry for greatness,
I have laser focus,
I will obtain everything positive I put my mind on,
I will receive promotions and raises, sales and commissions,
all my bills paid in full,
My business will grow,
I will find a way to make it happen,
I'm a survivor, a fighter, I am blessed,
I'm motivated and will motivate others,
I will achieve great things,
money will flow to me on a regular basis,
no one will break me or take my joy,
I'm in control, I'm secure and confident,
I will put this in action and have what I say....."

Stay in Your Lane

I always remember the image of Michael Phelps killing it in the Olympics while his opponent watched him push for the Gold medal. The picture itself tells a thousand words. His opponent lost focus on himself and took his eyes off the prize. Phelps was zoned in; he had a laser focus on what was in front of him. So, who won that race... you got it, the one with laser focus Mr. Phelps. In the Olympics, every split-second counts. As we gain experience through time, we realize this applies to our lives. Time is precious, and we cannot get it back. So, stop wasting time worrying about what other people are doing. No matter who you are or how much money you have, we all get 24 hours a day. That's why it's so important to make our time count. What are you doing with your 24? We should be spending a portion of it on self-improvement, so we can help ourselves and help others. Stay in your lane, be yourself, focus on you....oh and don't be a hater.

If everyone stayed in their lane and focused on themselves, there would be less chaos. Think about it! If you're someone who enjoys other people's success like myself, then negativity, hate, envy, and jealousy doesn't fit in your schedule. For instance, let's talk about social media. Recently I made a positive post on Facebook, and someone took my post and gave it a re-mix, then spewed out some negative comments and it didn't make sense. So, I deleted them rather than indulge in pettiness. Misery loves company, so stay away from it. Instead of getting mad, I prayed for this individual because obviously they're going through something.

Another example that comes to mind is Tai Lopez; he's an Entrepreneur who gives out a lot of good and sometimes free information. He's very successful, so why wouldn't you listen to what he has to say. Some information, classes or programs, you have to pay for. He has to make money, he's a businessman, so he provides services, and people pay for them, which they should. For one reason or another people hate on him, not all people but there always seems to be haters on his Facebook and Instagram. I think to myself wow, who has time to write so much trash and hate? If people spent their energy less on hating and more on their success, they would be better off. This isn't just Tai Lopez. There always seems to be someone complaining about someone or something. A friend of mine brought up a good point; he said look at all the YouTube videos there's always a handful of dislikes no matter what it is.

I couldn't imagine spending time going on people's sites and social media platforms and putting energy into negative criticism all day. Focus on yourself people, come on, wake up! If you're so unhappy with other people's content, then start making your own. Let's start putting out more good than bad. We also have to be geared up; we have to plow through the bad vibes and negative animosity; we have to go through life with a shield that protects us against anything thrown our way; let it bounce off, let it burn to dust, don't let that junk touch our greatness. You feel me?

When you want something, like a business, a new relationship, landing the job you want, making that deal, losing the weight, whatever it is, you have to become it! It has to become an obsession. That may sound crazy to some, but when I was building my business nothing could have gotten in my way. Things were thrown at me, but I kept it moving and had a laser focus on what was in front of me. I had specific goals written on paper and in my head. I found my inner me and tapped into my hunger. I barely slept because I wanted to go from ramen noodles to steak. This was my vehicle to get me rolling. Anything that's not in the plan or that takes you off course needs to be eliminated. Focus and become the vision. Don't make excuses, go out and get what's yours.

I have many friends and associates who have their own business. So, we get together from time to time analyze and compare notes. One of the same problems that seem to reoccur is worrying about the next Man/Woman's pay. It's been about eight years since I worked for someone, but when I did, I kept my head down and pushed forward. I never looked at the next person's pay or didn't bother to ask or care. Now you might be thinking well I have to know what people make so I can adjust or set a goal... yeah, yeah, yeah, I know. Just like I know what all my competition charges people, I get it. While some people are looking to see what the next person is doing, the person who has tunnel vision is doing laps and passing you twice. We need to focus on us and stop looking over and worrying about other people, that's how you get stuck. Concentrate on building yourself up and rising to the top. If you're doing great things and no one ever notices, then create your own lane, do it yourself. When you have a driving force, and you're doing what you need to do, nothing can stop you. I worked for tons of different companies and people. If you're getting treated right, that's one thing, but if you're not getting the recognition and pay you deserve, build your own lane, create it and enjoy what you build.

Think about the superhero Cyclops - when he shoots his laser out at a target, he smokes it. Laser Focus. Or when you're playing darts and hit the dead center bullseye. That's what you have to do in life when you want something or want to achieve a goal. If you're going to school and want a 4.0 grade, you have to fully commit and go for the taking. If you want to win a chicken wing eating contest, you've got to practice. Whatever it is in life you want, you have to decide to set a deadline and start moving. When you're wasting your energy and worried about the next man or woman, you're wasting your time. The most successful people have their own groove, their own way, their own vibe. I've shaken hands and broke bread with millionaires, entrepreneurs, pastors, Prophets, people with great morals and ethics. They all have their own pizzazz, they just are themselves and the energy flows. It's important to be yourself. I would love to be the life of the party like my brother-in-law, Josue; when he walks in a room, the fun starts. I'm more quiet and low key but also know how to enjoy myself. I love being me and thank GOD for being who I am. When you're honest and authentic everyone will gravitate to you, regardless of who you are.

I've learned many times not to judge another man or woman. Have I ever judged, sure I have, but every year I'm on this earth it's less and less. It's not fair to judge someone because you don't know what they're going through. If I ever start to judge I immediately question myself and say who you are to judge? I'll leave that in GOD'S hands. Remember, half the stories we hear are fabricated, amped up or remixed. Sometimes people sprinkle a little drama juice on top so that the story will sizzle. Come on! You know what I'm talking about, hahaha. This all correlates with staying in your own lane, if we spend less time judging and more time being focused there's less room for "he-said, she-said" gossip.

Matthew 7:3

"And why do you look at the speck in your brother's eye, but do not consider the plank in your own eye."

I'm pretty good at staying in my lane; however sometimes someone close needs to be told the truth. Now us as human beings should try and be encouraging and uplifting when telling someone the truth. It's not cool to kick someone when they're down. It's cool to help them up, help them through an addiction, help them break a habit, help them get that new job, or help put food on their table. Those types of things are greatness at its finest. Although, I must admit I'm very bold at times. There are certain situations where I don't beat around the bush. Sometimes we have to tell it how it is. Usually, it's to the closest people to us when we have to lay it out. What I'm saying is don't go around telling everyone what they need to be doing when you don't have it all together yourself. If you think you do, believe me, you don't. We all got some work to do on ourselves. It's not good to beat yourself up about it, but constant improvement should always be on our mind.

When you stay in your lane and focus, more opportunities will come. One of these is money. If you want to build and increase your wealth, then save at least 10% of your income. When you get paid, pay yourself first. This comes with focus and discipline. The more money you make, the higher percentage you should be saving. Then after it adds up, you invest it. I'm not a financial advisor so I can't tell you what to invest in, but I personally like real estate. It has good returns and has many advantages. For you, it might be something totally different. Let's say you make $800 a week then you would put at least 80 dollars aside in an envelope, account or whatever you choose and don't touch it until you accumulate enough to invest.

Some people say I can't do that I have too many bills and I have to do this and that. I understand, but if you don't pay yourself first, you may never get ahead. It takes discipline and laser focus to reach your goals. It could take six months or 4 years until you have enough to make a move but as long as you're saving for an investment you're moving in the right direction. I currently save 25% of everything I make. Then when I'm ready to make a move or when a business opportunity comes up to invest in, I'm ready. There's real estate, businesses, stocks, bonds, gold, silver, cryptocurrencies and much more. It's up to you to do your due diligence and do what makes you comfortable.

Also, if you don't have an IRA or some retirement fund, I suggest you start that as well. I have a Vanguard account, and they automatically withdraw money every month from my checking account, every month all year around. There's also the S&P 500 and so much more. I suggest you do your research and think about your future. Some people reading this may already know this, I'm just trying to be informative because we all have to learn at some point. I believe just holding money or keeping it in a savings account is weak, and you're losing. I would highly recommend researching to find a good investment that makes you a higher percentage on your money. So, spend some time thinking about your future and get started on investing in yourself.

There's a good book about this philosophy called the "Richest Man in Babylon" by George S. Clason. It explains and breaks down how it works. Also, Dan Lok talks about how to save and how much - check out his YouTube videos. I learn from the people making millions and the knowledge I've learned I'm just passing along. The more people we help, the higher we elevate. So, when you get paid, start paying yourself first and get started. I first learned this from Robert Kiyosaki who wrote all the RICH DAD, POOR DAD books. If you never start, you'll probably stay stuck. Paying yourself first becomes a habit, and you don't miss the money saved. You feel excited to save for your future investment.

I want to build hotels, buy apartment buildings, condos, build businesses, write more books and movies, travel to see the Pyramids and so much more. So, I read, watch, study, set up meetings and indulge in my visions. I observe my surroundings and watch how deals are being done, but I'm so focused on what I need to do that I don't care what the next person is doing. I pay attention and have a laser focus on me. I could care less what the next man is driving, wearing or eating. I don't care. I want people to succeed and do well. And that's a big part of my success. If you ever feel mad about someone's else's success, then you need to reevaluate where you are in life and ask yourself some questions. Like why am I mad, why am I hating, and what do I need to do to get back on track?

"Don't hate, congratulate!"

Set personal goals, and dream big! We can do anything in life with determination and a good attitude. Stay focused my friend.

Fuego – Let it Burn!

When the alarm goes off, don't hit the snooze button, don't lay back down, get up and get ready to dominate the day. There's a time to relax and a time to get busy. Yes, I know we are all created differently, and some of us have more ambition than others. What I can tell you is if you're looking for a way to live a better life financially, freely, and on your own terms then you have to have an urgency in the road to success. You have to eat, sleep, breathe, taste, touch and want success. No, it's not just money. Although that plays a big role for most, it's the freedom to be you; it's knowing you put in every fiber that's inside you toward a personal conquest. Success is a way of life, having fire is moving differently, walking, talking differently. You're not like the rest; you're cut from a different cloth. You have to let the fire burn deep, anything in your way that's creating a roadblock, burn it down. Let your passion and drive speak for itself. Be unstoppable.

"Everybody wants to be a beast until it's time to do
what real beasts do"
–Eric Thomas

To be successful, I mean at the top of the food chain, you have to have a fire inside (Fuego) that burns up everything you touch. When you touch a business, you go all in or don't go in at all. When my Pastor preaches, he spits fire. He lights the room up, and you feel the word of GOD. If you're cooking burgers, cook with fire. If you're doing nails, hair, eyelashes do it with fire. Tell all your customers you're the best, believe it and promote it. When you teach, you must teach with passion and heart. I'm not saying you have to be loud, what I'm saying is feel it, be passionate and let the room feel you when you speak. If you're learning something, be a sponge, ask questions, go early and spend extra time studying. You have to want it so bad that sleep is an inconvenience. You wake up Monday morning ready to fly and ready to burn. If you're hitting the snooze button, my friend, it's not fire; it's ice. You're cold; it's time to make a change and get motivated, heat it up, set some goals, be active.

We get one life on this Earth, as far as we know, so we need to dominate while we're here and make it happen. Enjoy yourself and have fun but, being on fire and having passion at what you love is important. If you're wondering what I'm talking about or are unsure what I'm saying I'll give you some examples. Let's say you're an artist and you paint pictures of beautiful landscapes. What I would do if you're starting is visit different landscapes around the world get inspired. If you can't afford it, do research, use Google, or find places in your area. Start drawing, painting consistently and constantly every day, nonstop. If you're serious about wanting to impact people and have an influence, then paint until your hand hurts, draw until your eyes are red. Now the most important time to paint is when you're uninspired, feeling lazy and your mind wants to make an excuse. Those are the times that separate the great from the average. When you don't want to do it, that's when it's necessary to get it in. Over time you'll start developing your own style and technique, and it will become second nature. People may start recognizing your work. But becoming good is half the battle now you gotta market yourself, get it out there and let the world see what you see. If you grind hard and have that fire inside you, eventually the seeds you plant will grow. Water with love. Everything depends on how much you put in. You have to go above and beyond. Go the extra mile. People like Michael Jordan didn't become extraordinary from doing average stuff. He went all out. First one there, last one to leave. It's important to be the best you can be at whatever it is you love to do.

I respect the karate teachers that teach the kids. My son is 5, and I have him learning self-defense. The instructors are great. They have patience, and you can tell they have a love for kids. Some people do social work and help people get back up on their feet, and there are those who help the homeless. I applaud everyone doing good in this world. When you're doing your work do it the best, be the best, don't shoot for mediocracy. Why be average when you can be extraordinary? Yes you, you can be the best at what you do. You have to want it and have fire while doing it. Nothing can stop you. It's a great feeling when you go all out and start to see the results of your hard work.

Proverbs 14:23

"Work brings profit, but mere talk leads to poverty!"

Listen, we have all have a story, and we should tell it. Life is a roller coaster and we all go through our ups and downs. One minute we're in Jamaica watching the sunset, the next day our car breaks down, and we lose our job. Whatever the situation is, we have to stay ready. That's why I stay prayed up, and why

I never try and get too comfortable. I wake up at 6 am and go to bed around 1 am every night. I'm constantly on the grind. There's always someone trying to take your spot. There's always someone working harder. So, it's imperative that you push forward and grind. Of course, enjoy the process and have fun doing it. Everyone won't agree that you need to grind every day and put in the hustle every day. And they're right. We all have different goals dreams and aspirations. For me personally; I come from a humble beginning. When I was 19, I got my own place and reality hit me in the face, but I loved it. When we're out there alone, that's when we grow. I've eaten at the most beautiful restaurants, and I've had nights where I didn't eat at all. I went through ups and downs, highs and lows. Life is a journey, and I believe we should enjoy it all. **Our toughest moments of adversity are the moments that build our character.**

When I was around 24 years old, I dug myself a deep, I mean deep, hole. I was off balance. I was broke, frustrated and full of uncertainty. I had credit cards maxed out - everything under the sun I owed. Through my hardship, I never blamed anyone, I was more upset with myself for putting myself in that position.

On top of that, I couldn't afford the gas for my house and it got shut off. Without gas, I had no hot water for a year straight. I live in Buffalo NY, and in the winters, it gets cold, brick cold. I used to be able to see my breath in my house. After work, I would have to take freezing showers, talk about humbling. That's why I'm so grateful for everything I have. Every morning I thank GOD for my blessings, every sip of coffee, every hot shower is a blessing. At that time, there were nights I didn't eat. My cousin is an infantryman, a true soldier, so he taught me how to survive. When you have a soldier with you who fought in Iraq and Afghanistan, nothing seemed too hard. How can I complain when he was the definition of a warrior? I got myself in this position from making a lot of bad decisions. So, I don't tell this story to make my life sound sad, because it wasn't sad, I learned a lot from making the wrong decisions.

I was making music at the time which I thought was going to pay me and it did, but not very much. I did complete two full albums and did tons of shows. It was fun, and I put in the effort, but it just wasn't paying the bills. I was spending too much money on going out to the clubs and not enough time focusing. It was my fault I was in this position. I look back, and I should have been more resourceful, I should have searched for a mentor or someone to help me, but I believe going through my trials and tribulations helped build the man I am today.

I'm going to give you a little insight on how I grew up, so you know where I'm coming from. My pops wasn't in the picture. When I started hanging with him, I was around 16-17. He wasn't what you call your everyday role model. When I got my license that's when I started to visit him. He lived a wild life traveling and living it up in his younger years. When I started to hang with him, he would give me champagne and whatever else he had and said, here drink this, take this. I'm the complete opposite with my son and step kids. It is what it is, that's just the way it was. I respect him for his work ethic though - he worked on the railroad for 30 years and got his pension. He also holds records for weightlifting as well. He was a go-getter, but unfortunately, I don't remember too much of him in my childhood. I'm happy we got to spend some time in Arizona before he passed away. I will tell you what though, we had some crazy nights. I love my dad and miss him. RIP. With that said, I didn't have the father figure I really needed.

My mom and stepdad were always there for me but the life I was living at the time kept me distant. My mom was awesome growing up, she always taught me good morals and showed me how to treat people. She used to give the kids in the neighborhood money to go to the movies and shared everything. She's a giver. My mom has an entrepreneurial spirit. She used to cut hair in our apartment growing up, and I watched her make her money. I thought that was cool! We didn't have much financially, but we always had food on the table. Sunday was that good Italian Sauce. We had great Christmases and lots of love. There were times the lights got cut off, and we struggled, but hey, it built me tough. Growing up with challenges made me mentally strong, I wouldn't change anything. We never had a car growing up which was fine because we rode our bikes everywhere. My mom and I were best friends and had tons of fun together.

Back then food stamps weren't on a card, they were paper like dollars, but they stood out, and it was embarrassing. If another kid saw you with food stamps, they would make fun of you. We were on welfare, and I knew as a kid I never wanted to be on welfare when I got older. I know it wasn't easy raising me by herself, but she did it. She gives me the strength I have today. We lived in a low-income apartment complex, but my school had a lot of rich kids there. It was a really good school, and I'm thankful I got to go there. I remember thinking one day I'm going to drive a nice car and have a big house. A couple of my friends which I still speak to this day would have me sleep over, and their houses blew my mind. Their parents were so nice to me and would take me to all type of places. I would go on their boat, go to amusement parks and I was always fed well. I believe this had a psychological effect on me. It made me want more than the life I was living. I was only 12 but growing up seeing my friends living in the houses they lived in inspired me as a young boy.

My step pops Larry came in my life when I was 10 and became a father figure when I was about 15. He bought a house and me and my mom moved in. I know it wasn't easy for him because I have step kids now and you have to step into a new role. I love it though; my step kids mean the world to me. He gave me some good lectures about life that sunk in years later. By him talking to me rather than yelling, his words always sunk in. He was very calm in a lot of situations; it rubbed off on me in many ways. I appreciate the wisdom and love they both gave me.

So now you have an idea of my upbringing and understand where my hunger and fire to succeed come from. There were a lot of seasons I did well and seasons that I struggled. I was struggling at this particular time, but I'm not the type of person to lay my problems on someone else, especially when I was the reason for being in that situation. I always worked and hustled and did what I had to do, and there were times I had money, but this season was rough for me. I knew I had to make some changes, All I needed was an opportunity. I was tired of the debt, the lifestyle, I wanted to be on top. I was willing to work for it and go all in. If I got a chance, I would go hard.

I remember walking down the street one night and saying, *"GOD, I know there's got to be more to life than this. I know I'm in this position because of my own doing, and I'm not asking for you to bail me out because I don't deserve it. All I want, all I pray for is an opportunity. If you can bless me with that one thing, I'll bust my butt and get out of this mess. Thank you, GOD."* That night I don't know what it was, but I felt different. Soon after, my brother got a job with his friend and stepdad. They owned a roofing company. He eventually got me a job too, and I was making good money. I did hard labor; my body used to be so sore and my feet would be killing me. But I didn't care because I was hungry. Hungrier than anyone in the world I felt. I busted my butt. I labored for a couple of years; then I learned how to roof. The more I learned, the more I got paid. My body was sore, but I loved it. I was working outside making money, and I felt alive. I started watching the bosses and observed how they operated. I would go on estimates with the one owner sometimes and watch him with the customers. He was really good. He made them feel comfortable.

I got an opportunity to move in with a great friend who I consider a brother now, Tone. I knew I had to make a change because of the atmosphere I was in. That's a big part of the reason I wasn't excelling; the atmosphere and people around me were keeping me stagnant. They were making choices that were not healthy. I knew it was my time to shine but that atmosphere was holding me back.

The day I moved in with Tone it was on. We both had the same vision and were on the same track for success. By the way, our cottage house was the size of a lunchbox - super small. We had our own rooms; the living room was a studio where we recorded music. There was a tiny bathroom and a tiny kitchen, but those were some of the best times. The best part is the bills were super cheap, haha. Tone saw me making some dough with the roofing, he was doing his thing with music, but we started to see a vision with the roofing game. We had a great vibe together and kicked it and we decided to start our own contracting business. We didn't know much as far as the business side, but it didn't matter. We went and got our DBA and believed in a vision.

Now more than ever was the time to pay close attention, especially to the business aspect. I told the owner of the company I was working for that we had started our own business and everyone kind of laughed it off, but it didn't matter. We were focused and had fire. We had a deal with him where if we landed a job, we would split it three ways between us. So, what I would do every single day, seven days a week was a grind. I would do a roof for my boss, then get out, take a shower and hit the road with Tone. We would go door to door and ask people if they needed roofing, gutters or siding done. We would knock on doors until dark. We wouldn't go home until we got at least five estimates. We were the definition of hungry. Try roofing in the sun for 8 hours then knocking on doors until dark. It's physically and mentally draining, but I did it. I did it with fire. I knew I had no choice but to succeed. I never once thought, "What if I fail?" Honestly, it never crossed my mind. I couldn't fail because I was working harder than anyone I ever met in my life. I never met anyone, at that moment of time, who was doing what I did. I was a straight animal. I never slept. My friends were partying at the beach and wanted me to come party. I said, "I can't go, guys, I'm knocking on doors, and I'm grinding." Two years of knocking, it sucked for me at first, I hated it. I forced myself to do something I never dreamed I would do. But when you're desperate to be successful, you'll knock, believe me. Although I didn't like doing it, I faked myself into it; I pretended I liked it. And did it with a smile. It was nerve-racking, people asked me questions I didn't know and asked for references I didn't have. They all said you look too young to have your own business. I was battling all types of things. But Tone and I kept fighting and pushing and not taking no for an answer. We were persistent. We would call these people for a year straight, and most of them never let us do anything. But through all of this, I learned how to take rejection, eat it up and spit it out. If you can't take denial or rejection, you better learn quickly because the road to success isn't for the weak hearted. I've been denied so many times in my life it doesn't affect me anymore. I take the lesson and move forward.

Think about the NBA where you have to have a short-term memory. If you make a bad play, there's no time to dwell on it, you've got to get back and play. I also learned to fear nothing. I would get home exhausted but had such joy and happiness every night. I knew eventually I would break through. We finally landed a roofing job. We did an awesome job, and the homeowners were happy. I remember driving home late that night so proud of us. Proud of myself for digging deep and the GLORY of GOD was all over me. GOD gave me that opportunity which I will always be grateful for, and I ran with it. I still remember the feeling of accomplishment and the feeling of hard work paying off. We eventually got so busy that we went on our own. Fast forward ten years later, we have a very successful company and do amazing work throughout all of western New York. All that hard work we put in opened other opportunities that I would have never dreamed of. I learned a great deal about real estate and properties, which helped me buy my first rental. I've met some great people, customers and contractors. I'm truly blessed and thankful. I have a true love, and a passion for real estate and through the grace of GOD will own thousands of properties.... That's my goal!

Now when I do estimates, I go in the sale knowing I'm going to land it. I have no doubt. Do I land every job? No. But I do pretty dang good. We do quality work and give very fair prices. I feel like I'm the best out here and my competition won't outwork me. Some people like to bid a job last because they feel like they'll come in and have an advantage. I couldn't disagree more. I want to be first every time. I feel like they could have ten people coming and it wouldn't matter, because I will close the deal being the first one there. I connect with people; when I get a call, I'm at their house within two days. A lot of times if possible, I go the day I get the call. People love that! I know that if I need something done and the person gets right to me, it shows a lot about their character.

You have to want it though. If I put off a sale, then the next guy who's hungry will come in and swoop out from right under me. I feel like I'm the hungriest out here. You have to have the attitude of a go-getter. If you let people break you down or distract you, then your falling in the trap. Be hungry, think big, go hard, push forward, go all out, have thick skin, let them talk while you count your money, let them hate while you build an empire. It doesn't matter what you do or where you are in life, you can be the best and you can dig your way out. If you're a cook, then cook your butt off, let people say man that's the best burger I ever had. If you're a waitress, let people say she was the best server ever, she was so polite, funny and enthusiastic. If you're in the hole, start digging, chip away, have a fire to get out. If I did it, I know you can. I had absolutely nothing. Now I have successful businesses, real estate and a handful of investments — many streams of income.

But most importantly I have a great relationship with GOD. I have a beautiful fiancée, Benita, my son, step kids and a handful of good friends. I'm a happy man, and I worked hard to get where I am, and I'm not going back. Progress and move forward. If you're going to do it.... do it with fire.

Smell the Roses

When things are getting heavy, and my mind is on overflow, I love to go alone to the water and just be at peace and let myself go. Kill the noise and chaos, and let my mind be free. Turn off the phone and just zone out. The sound of the waves and the smell of the water is a beautiful feeling. The water always takes me to a place of gratitude and a place of strength. You can leave all your problems there, think about them for the last time and let them go. It's good to get yourself together. Some of my greatest ideas, plans, visions come from a form of peace and meditation. You don't have to do any breathing techniques or anything in that way... just be at one with the Earth and with yourself. Enjoy it. Think about all the things you're grateful for — all the things you want to accomplish. Believe me; I know life gets hard, the world weighs a ton, but we have to keep pushing. Some people may enjoy the mountains, music, the gym, whatever your release is, whatever takes you to the place where you need to be is the place you should go and go often!

A few years back I was walking through the mall with my stepdaughter and I received a text from my fiancée asking, "Who did you go to the movies with?" She had found a ticket stub and she thought I went to the movies with someone. I thought it was funny at the time, but she didn't. See, what she didn't realize is every so often if I really want to see a movie, I go by myself. Yeah, that's right, by myself. I also take walks by myself, go out to breakfast by myself and do many other things by myself. What she thought was something strange at first, she now does herself. She takes time for herself, which she should. My lady likes to go to Red Lobster and hang out from time to time. She made a couple of friends with the waitresses and formed a bond just from spending time alone. When you're always on the grind and hustling and moving, it's important to slow down for a moment and smell the roses. Life moves fast; we're here then we're gone. You might ask yourself, he just said to hustle and have fire, and now he's saying slow down and enjoy life. Yes, that's what I'm saying. It's important to be alone sometimes. Get your thoughts together go into prayer. Be at one with yourself. Meditate or just reflect on your life and what's to come, your vision for the future, your goals. Double down on your loved ones and people that are making a positive impact on your life. They are rare and don't come around often. Sometimes we take close family and friends for granted, and that's not good. We have to acknowledge the people who lift us up, because they're unique and special. Nowadays it seems many people have an angle or want something from you. You should have a good idea of the people dragging you down, slowing you up or putting negative thoughts around you. When we have negative people around us, we have to walk away. It's hard, but it's the best move you can make. Sometimes it's someone close to us, and we feel bad, but it's like a dark rain cloud every time you're with them. I'm not saying abandon your family or turn your back, what I'm saying is limit the time your spending with people who aren't elevating you. They say you are who you hang with so think about who you're spending most of your time with. If someone is poisoning you, you're going to have to make a move or limit the time you spend with that person. Don't take any abuse, be strong and rise above everything and anything you have to.

It's the little things in life! I think we can all agree there have been times in life when we feel like no one cares or you're not getting enough credit, or your work isn't getting the recognition it deserves. Whatever it may be. It is what it is — we have to roll with it. Life isn't all peaches; we have to be strong, have thick skin and keep pounding forward. So, when someone does something nice for me, I pay extra attention, and I can decipher real from fake. It can be as little as an honest compliment or someone buying me a pack of pens. Little things go a long way with me — also, the little things in life I pay attention to. When we're going 100 miles an hour, sometimes we overlook the beauty that's right in front of us.

I love the sunset. When I was in Jamaica, it was extraordinary. There was nothing like it. It reset my thought process. When I pick my son up from school, and he runs towards me smiling, that's all I need. There's no materialistic thing that can replace unconditional love. I come from a humble beginning, so I'm just so grateful for everything GOD has blessed me with. My back has been against the wall, and I've learned to leave it in GOD's hands, and he's never failed me. He always comes through every time. It may not be the way we want it to work out, but it's not up to us. GOD doesn't put you through what you can't handle.

I find a good way to keep yourself on point is to take something away from yourself for some time. That's why I like fasting a couple of times a year. That's something you should consult your doctor with. I drink nothing but water for a few days, sometimes with lemon. There are some people who do it once a week. Some people do it for weeks. We're all different. But when you fast you become one with yourself and GOD. You reach levels that normally you don't reach. Physically, spiritually, emotionally and mentally. When I do it, I eat fruits and vegetables for two days, then only fruit for a day, then I go into fasting. But everyone is different, so you should get professional advice before you do it. When I went on my diet for six weeks, I gave up pizza, wings, bread, alcohol, pop, sweets. I ate chicken, oatmeal, eggs, tuna, vegetables, shakes and fruits, and a ton of water.

After I accomplished my goal I went and got pancakes. Man, those were good! It's good to give up something once in a while so you can feel in control. A lot of things we take for granted until we don't have a choice. When I was 19, I broke my right hand. I had a cast the whole summer. I'm right handed, so I had to learn how to do everything left-handed. It was challenging, but I learned some valuable lessons along the way.

It's important to pay attention to detail and acknowledge the people in our life and the world going on around us, as much as possible. When a child says, "Mom, dad look what I made," it's important we take the time and pay attention and show we care, especially for kids. When we show recognition and joy for our kids when they achieve something, it builds their confidence. I build my son up; I teach him how to be humble, but confident. He may not completely understand, but it's in the subconscious mind. I keep planting the seed. I believe it's up to us as parents to leave our kids better off than we were. I'm talking morals, ethics, treating people with respect, and passing the knowledge to the younger generation.

Another way to open your mind is to learn about different cultures and travel to different places. I love traveling. I've been blessed to travel to many places. I've met great people along the way and had some awesome memories and cool stories. What I'm saying is get out there and be yourself and enjoy life. Do the things you always wanted to. Take time for you. Sometimes we concentrate so much on everyone else we forget about ourselves, and that's not good. Take time, do your facials, nails, hair, exercise, travel, explore, try different foods, color, draw, build, lift, sing, talk, teach, preach, cook, learn, take classes and seminars, ride, play in the mud, swim, love, do everything you can.... And do it with joy!

"One of the most tragic things I know about human nature is that all of us tend to put off living. We are all dreaming of some magical rose garden over the horizon instead of enjoying the roses that are blooming outside our windows today"
—Dale Carnegie

Good Spirit:
Energy & Atmosphere

I understand we're all different which is awesome. Imagine if we were all the same, how boring life would be. I'm sharing some of the ways I move. You may agree or disagree with my techniques or way of life which is fine. I'm just trying to help people who want to get the most out of their day and be in a positive mindset and create their atmosphere.

When I wake up and open my eyes every morning, I feel blessed. *Ahhhh another day!! Thank you, GOD!* I go into my office, get on my knees and give thanks for another day, give thanks for all my blessing's. I've been through so many challenges and faced so much opposition, no matter what GOD has always had my back and pulled me through. For me, building a relationship with GOD is the most important relationship in my life.

We are here on earth then we're gone, it flies faster than we think. Did you know according to quora.com 53.3 million people die every year? 151,600 people die every day. Just waking up should be enough of a reason to feel grateful. I hear so many people complaining, I just don't get it. To me, it's just wasted energy and wasted time.

I love waking my 5-year-old son up for school, seeing my step kids looking good, saying good morning to Benita and everything that comes with it. That first sip of coffee, oh boy it's good, I enjoy every sip. I rise early because my phone starts ringing at 6:30 a.m. and doesn't stop until 10 pm. I have to be prepared for anything and everything. Like I said, I own a contracting business, and I'm invested in a couple of other businesses and own real estate. There's never a dull day. I give GOD my gratitude then I pray for the strength to endure any situation that comes my way. I stay Prayed up! I constantly and consistently pray throughout the day. It's equipping yourself with armor for any attack against you. The happier you are, the more you will be attacked. There are not too many people who will tell you this, but it's the truth. The enemy will try to steal, kill and destroy anything and everything you have. Have you ever noticed when you're in a great mood someone will show up and try to throw you off? It's like, *Dang stay out my zone,* right? Back in the day, I would fight fire with fire and come right back. I would let people take me out of character. Now I handle things differently. I'm more passive and let things roll off me. I don't let people bother me as much, but I'm not a pushover either.

Every situation calls for a different response. I understand life can be difficult and sometimes it's tough just to smile and walk away. There are levels to the game, and sometimes that's what it is – a game. I know a certain individual who used to press my buttons, but over time his methods got less and less effective, until he gave up. A lot of times people go through life miserable and mad at the world, and so they want to take you with them. Don't let them. If you're at peace with yourself, prayed up with GOD, and have a good positive attitude, you should be ready for anything. Here's a Gem for you! Let's say someone texts you something foul and they are coming at you. Some people would reply so fast the auto correct couldn't keep up. There's a saying "Don't react.... respond.":

We should always take our time and analyze the situation before responding if possible. Think about the scenario and what the outcome of your reaction or response could be. You can fire right back, but that usually brings more animosity. Take your time before you respond... breathe, take a walk, then come back to the situation. Being cool and calm is the best solution in almost every case. However, there are times when that won't work. I think outside the box and address real-life situations. There are some people who act like you can be positive in every situation. Well, if you're living on planet Earth that's just not true. However, there are ways to deal with people who are trying to take you out of character.

"Great spirits have always encountered violent op-
position from mediocre minds"
−Albert Einstein

In Brazilian jiu-jitsu and other martial arts, they teach you how to avoid fights with peace. They don't do this because they're weak, they do it because they're strong and educated mentally and physically. If you decide to go against a black belt in Brazilian jiu-jitsu you won't come out looking so tough. However, these are trained professionals and most likely they will put you in a submission hold make you look foolish and tell you to have a nice day. If they wanted to, they could break your arms and legs in 10 different places. Most of the time it would never come to that. I would suggest if you're in a place where things are getting funky and out of control, to simply leave and get out. I try not to even put myself in a negative atmosphere, and when I walk in a place, if I'm not feeling it, I don't stay long. Especially when there's alcohol involved. What I'm saying is keep yourself out of harm's way, go to places where there's opportunity and a good atmosphere. I'm not saying I never have a beer because that would be a lie, what I'm saying is think about where you're putting yourself, and what type of atmosphere are you going to be around. The more time you spend in positive places the less of a chance of a serious altercation. It's better when we surround ourselves with good people and a good environment.

Sometimes I like to have a beer and a taco and keep it moving. What I've come to realize though is that time is the most valuable asset we have, so use it wisely. The best weapon is to stay busy; for me that's writing, reading, learning and making moves. Try to Surround yourself with greatness and people who are making moves. Improvement every day is key.

Progress and move forward, constantly put things in your mind that help you get better and teach you things. Watch YouTube videos, and listen to audios, and good music. I love music with a passion, but if I played music all day, I wouldn't get as much accomplished. Some suggestions on YouTube are Eric Thomas, Inky Johnson, Gary V, Les Brown, Jim Rohn, Joel Osteen, TD Jakes, Billy Alsbrooks, Tony Robbins, and Zig Ziglar. Also, you should be reading. Some people don't like reading, and that's ok, but try to read ten pages a day. You're chipping away at knowledge — little by little.

The most important instrumental book to me is the Bible. A lot of people don't realize that vast wisdom and knowledge comes from the Bible. If you're not familiar with the Bible, start with Proverbs. Proverbs has amazing insight, and one verse can get you through the day. What elevated my way of thinking was going to Bible study. The way my Pastor Alberto De Leon breaks down the Word is incredible. I've been going for five years now, and it has had a major impact on the way I treat others and walk on this journey of life. Studying under such an amazing man has helped shape my inner me. When you start to feel and experience the Holy Spirit, your life will change. The Holy Spirit guides you through life and helps you feel the direction you're supposed to go.

When I talk to someone wrong, I feel it. If I make the wrong move, I feel it. Whenever I'm off track, I immediately know. I have to try and make the situation right, or I'm not myself. I don't mind apologizing if I'm wrong. I've been wrong thousands of times, and I'll be wrong again, but it's important to me to try and make it right. The Holy Spirit tells you in your gut when you walk in a room and something isn't right. Follow your gut, follow your instincts, follow what you feel to be right. The Holy Spirit guides you and I want to make people aware of the power it has and its presence.

I have way more experiences in a good atmosphere and with good people because I walk with a good spirit a good inner self. People who have a good spirit gravitate to each other. Why do you think we stop hanging with certain people? The higher you elevate, the more you find yourself with people on the same energy level. It's not because you're better than other people. It's because you start hanging with people who have the same type of dreams, the same type of goals, the same type of mindset and the same type of determination to succeed.

I'm no saint. 1st Timothy Ch 1:15 "Jesus came in this world to save sinners, and I am the chief." I don't claim to be perfect.

However, by consistently continuing to progress and push forward, GOD has been chiseling my mind, body, and soul to become better and stronger. Sometimes to reach the mountains, you must let certain people in your life go. It may be a girlfriend/boyfriend, coworker, parent, friend, sister, brother whatever the case may be. Sometimes you have to let go to progress to the next level. It's tough, I know, but if you don't, it can stagnate you spiritually, mentally, physically, emotionally and financially. I had to cut certain people out my life because of this, and ever since I did it, it's been a better place for me in every way shape and form.

If you're looking for positive energy books, "Think and Grow Rich" by Napoleon Hill is a book that changed my thought process. I read it when I was about age 26 and from there on my way of thinking has always been positive. I watched the movie "The Secret" which was about the law of attraction. There are some great people in there like Bob Proctor, Jack Canfield, and others. I wanted to dig deeper, and I found a lot came from Dale Carnegie. When you read the Bible there are powerful scriptures in there, such as Matthew 7:7 "Ask and it will be given to you; seek and you will find; knock and the door will be opened to you." When you start to dig for knowledge, it gets exciting and opens doors. I suggest you try. Check out books by Dale Carnegie such as "How to Win Friends & Influence People." The book "Richest Man in Babylon" taught me how to accumulate wealth. Jack Canfield's book "Law of Attraction." If you're going into real estate, Robert Kiyosaki taught me a lot. He taught me a new way of thinking as far as good debt, bad debt, and cash flow. I suggest getting all his "Rich Dad Poor Dad" books. Grant Cardone is also really good for learning real estate. Whatever field or business you're looking to get into, the knowledge is there. You just have to make an effort and get it.

When you wake up, listen to things that get you motivated – things that give you fire. When you go to bed, listen to positive things that put you at ease and level you out. It's very important. Our subconscious mind will start gravitating towards all the good you're taking in and feed you back greatness. Read books by Bob Proctor on the power of the "subconscious mind." I think back when I was in hardship, broke, confused and cold. I was listening to junk, talking junk, and putting too much liquor and beer in my body. Feed your mind good things like inspirational books, positive videos and have intellectual conversations. Feed your body with healthy foods, fruits, vegetables, and lots of water. Exercise: try and sweat a few times a week at least. If you don't like the gym, at least run or walk around the block a few times a week... it's easy and free. In the morning, give thanks to GOD for another day. Meditate, get your mind right before you go out in the world and stay prayed up. Being grateful and giving thanks is so important, it's crucial to your happiness. All of my studies go to this place of being grateful and giving thanks to all your blessings. Gratitude is key. The kindest people I've ever met are the ones who show appreciation.

What you put out is what you get in return. If you're happy and lift people up, it will come back to you. If you help someone elevate, someone will help you elevate. If you give money, money will come to you 10-fold. It's just how it works. The more you give, the more you receive. There have been times where I've advised friends about real estate, and the very next day I met someone who taught me new things about real estate I had no idea about. It came back fast. I love to give to people who are in need. I love to give money to people who don't know it's coming. Seeing the joy on their face and happiness is enough to keep me going for a lifetime. If you don't have the money to give, then spend time with people or an organization. When I give money, it might be a woman with kids walking down the street pushing a cart. I pray for guidance and my heart leads me to the people I should give to. In the Bible, it says you should tithe 10% of your profits. The people who don't give are the people who are usually broke minded. I've heard all the arguments against giving, and I've seen the evidence. The people who are most successful are the ones that give. How can GOD trust you with millions if you can't give a few dollars to help someone eat? Where and how you give your money is exclusively up to you. I would say follow your heart. Buy someone a coffee, breakfast, lunch, a coat, a motel for the night, shoes, books, tuition or whatever it may be. I can make you a promise: when you give unexpectedly to someone and see and feel the joy on their face, there's no other feeling like it, not drugs, alcohol or anything else. Your spirit is lifted, and it feels great.

Now when you give you don't have to let the whole world know and blow your trumpet.

Matthew 6:2 "so when you give to the needy, do not announce it with trumpets, as the hypocrites do in the synagogues and on the streets, to be honored by others. Truly I tell you, they have received their reward in full."

Yes, there are times when it's good to inspire others and show the world it's good to give. However, if you buy someone groceries so they can eat, there's no need for you to post it on Facebook and say, "Look what I did." There's a time and place for everything. Your blessings come back when you give from the heart, not when you're giving for attention from others, so you can look good. If that's your intention, then you may as well not give at all. However, if you're showing the world what you're doing and it's from the heart, then you're all good. It's good to help someone learn, to teach them what you know, to volunteer for kids and the elderly. If anyone asks me for advice or knowledge, I'm happy to tell them my input and try to inspire them to be at their full potential.

I love giving to my Church; when I come out of Church or Bible study, I feel new, elevated and more intelligent about the Word. I've had personal experiences that no one on the planet could take away. I promise you every year I'm getting better, and GOD is working with me, in every aspect of life. I want to show people how I'm going to the next level. It's a long process, but I can see the mountaintop.

When I was 29, I gave $1,000 to my good friend who was helping teenagers and teaching the Word. Some of the kids didn't have much money. I put my trust in him and said here's some money; GOD put it in my heart to give this to you, and I want you to give it to a student who's in need. He said wow! He was very grateful, and he said he would get back to me. A few days later, he said, "Here's what I did, I split it into 4 separate scholarships for books." He said the students were taking classes and needed books. So, I got to go to lunch with these four young women and men. They were amazing people. They were very grateful, and we had an amazing lunch. I shared that story to give you ideas or insights on how to give. (There's been times I gave or helped and only me, that person and GOD knows, and that's how I usually like it).

Find a Way

W ake up! We've got one life here on earth as far as
we know, so make a move...

*Do something you love, create, be great,
fight through, speak, preach, teach, help others, get
it, do it, grind, work, shine, one more step, just a little more, push, stay calm, forgive, let it go, be driven,
have fire, take the high road, be understanding, survive, breakthrough, there's victory inside you, you
are blessed, you are awesome, stay motivated, have
a purpose, believe, love yourself, put GOD first, elevate, keep it moving and no matter how hard it gets,
find a way.*

I have a drive inside me and a fire that burns deep. I know
what it's like to have the lights cut off. I know what it's like not
to eat, to take cold showers, no heat, repossessed cars, $65,000
in debt and to feel empty inside. I used to go out and drink and
waste too much time. I look back and I'm thankful I'm still here
because I was wild and been through some crazy stuff. It's
funny because I'm the opposite now, I'm laid back and calm. I
also can't stand clubs now; I'd rather be chilling with my son at

the park drinking a coffee or hanging with Benita and step kids. My point is I know what it was like to be messed up and living in chaos. I'm sure we all have had our moments. No matter what happened to me in life, I refused to blame someone else for my mistakes, or my faults. That's an easy way out; it's a poor excuse. I believe greatness comes from truth and the willingness to accept responsibility for your actions. Greatness comes from the ability to find a way out of the mess you created. I fought hard for years to get out of debt; it wasn't easy, but I chipped away. I dug deep and found a way to progress and push through and dominate everything I put my heart, mind and soul into. I do my best when my back's against the wall. I can become really creative; it's a skill I've learned over time. One second left, give me the ball I'll take the shot. How about you? Do you need to strengthen yourself when the situation gets tough? When the heat is on, how do you handle the stress and pressure? Sometimes being thrown in the fire is the best way to learn, when we're right in the middle.

"You need to pave your own way in the world"
–Lori Greiner

It takes you to be uncomfortable to really know how you'll perform. It's good to do uncomfortable things that we're not used to; it makes us better. We're not perfect, and we will fail sometimes, but when we fail, fail forward. Some people look at failure as a great loss. I look at it as a learning experience; I get back on my feet, wipe off the dust and move forward. Enjoy it – don't take it so seriously. Life is crazy, I can promise you that. We just have to try our best and keep it moving.

When I was 15 years old, my mother said, "Matthew (only my mom calls me that), put on your khakis, a button down shirt and a tie, and go apply to some jobs." I said, "Ok mom," and off I went. During my second interview, I got hired on the spot. It was the Family Tree restaurant. I still eat there to this day; the chicken souvlakis are the best. I got hired as a busboy, and I cleaned up dishes off the tables, wiped them down and loaded them in the back at the dishwasher. At the end of the night, I would get tipped out by the waitresses.

I saved up enough money that year to buy a hooptie, that's a beat-up car in case you didn't know. It got me from A to B, so I didn't care what it looked like. That summer, gas was only around a dollar a gallon – those were the days! One Friday night it was slammed in there. I was sweating, emptying the dishes out my bus pan and looked over and saw piles of dishes like a mountain; I thought what the heck is going on? I asked the dishwasher, and he said the dishwasher broke. I looked over, and saw the owner of the restaurant rolling up his sleeves and proceed to wash the dishes by hand. People were freaking out and nervous because it was so busy, and they needed plates and silverware, but he was calm and collected. He never said anything, just reacted to the situation. He was busting those dishes out. As a 15-year-old I was young, but I recognized the situation and had a new respect for that man. He got it done. This may not seem like a big deal, but it had a profound effect on me and still does to this day in the way I run my business. I don't stand around and wait, I attack the problem and do whatever it takes.

You have to be ready for whatever, whenever in business and life. While working there, I also learned the word "improvise". It's incredible how some things we never forget. I was bussing tables with another guy who was a little older than me. He did it for extra cash. He was a cool dude. We were working and ran out of some things needed for the job, and he said we're going to have to improvise. I said, "What is improvise?" And he showed me how to use something that wasn't meant for the task. It was simple, what we needed was a strainer, but we didn't have one. It caught all the garbage so that it wouldn't go down the drain. So he used something similar laying in the back. He then explained what it meant and showed me as well. I thought to myself, thank you for that lesson. Anytime someone teaches me something, I'm so grateful. Little things mean a lot to me. I still remember that so well. It's important that we know how to improvise. We may not have the right tools, or the right people, or the this or that, but use what you have and make it happen. It's not always easy and there will be times we've got to roll up our sleeves. Just don't quit, don't complain. Find a way and get it done.

"Find a way, Guariglia, find a way…" That was Coach Gross pushing me to my absolute limit. He was my sophomore basketball coach. It was his first-year coaching at our school Amherst High, and boy did he make a statement. We had a secret signal: if you grabbed your shorts and wiggled them, that meant you were tired and needed to come out of the game. I tried doing that and Coach Gross would look dead at me and turn around and ignore me. He got every last bit out of me he could. I was in the best shape of my life as far as cardio. We practiced so hard that when it was game time, we were ready to kill it. Those three words stick in my head to this day: "find a way." I apply it to my life in every aspect. I haven't seen Coach in years, but I'll be happy to give him a copy of this book when I see him. You're in debt…find a way, can't pay your bills, find a way, need a car, find a way, need a job, find a way, want a house, find a way, whatever it is you seek, find a way. No more excuses. Take responsibility and **find a way** to get what you are going after.

Anything I ever wanted, I had a fire to get it. I realized that no one on this planet was going to do it for me. I wasn't given any money and didn't have people teaching me about business. I had to study, trial and error, seminars, meetings, I watched, studied people who were doing what I wanted and created my own lane. There were nights I didn't get sleep because there was just too much to do. We are all different, but I like to study and write during the night. My son is asleep, my step-kids are sleep, my lady is chilling, and I can concentrate on the things that need to get done. I zone out at night and get a lot of work done. By work, I mean study time and writing time, knowledge for self.

The only way I was going to learn about real estate was to dive in. I found ways on my own, also books, audios and anyone who would answer my questions. I will never stop asking questions. Anyone who has anything to do with real estate, I'm interested in speaking with. It's awesome how things fall into place when you put in the work. All Glory to GOD. I believe GOD will put things in front of us, but it's up to us to execute the plan. We have to move to it. We can't sit and just hope things happen. We have to get off our butt and make it happen. Action!

"So also, faith by itself, if it does not have works, is dead."
James 2:17.

At one point I was living in South Buffalo. I was roofing and didn't have a car and needed one badly. I was working off the books at the time so I wasn't able to provide a pay stub. There was a '97-Grand Prix for sale across the street in a lot; it was a turquoise green color. Not the Grand Am that got repossessed, this was a different car. It was dope. I said *dang that's sweet*, I looked at it, but didn't pay much mind to it. The next day I saw it and said *Man, that's a dope car.* This happened for about a week; then I finally said *Man, that's my car! I'm going to buy it. I don't know how, but it's mine.* Finally, I walked over and talked to a young salesperson. I told him my situation, and he said I had to talk to the owner at the shop. So, I went to talk to him. It was about $6,000 for the car. I had $800 saved up. I had no proof of income and didn't know anyone to vouch for me at that time. All I owned was an old beat up van. I walked up to the owner and said, "Hi, my name is Matty Guariglia, I make this much a week, I have $800 to put down and an old van I could trade in." He said, "Are you sure you can make the payments?" I replied, "Not only am I sure, I'm going to pay that car off faster than you can blink." He said, "Sure, I'll give you a shot, let's do it." I was driving it the next day. I'm not going to lie – it took courage. I had never done anything like that before. However, that opened a door for me, and I never looked back. It made me face the fear of rejection, denial or whatever else I was thinking. I was rolling in my Pontiac Grand Prix like it was a brand-new Ferrari. I found a way. The way I found, was just doing it.

Go for it. As an experienced salesman, business owner and investor, I now eat rejection and spit it out. I'm not scared to get denied or rejected. I believe we all have a moment where we say, *You know what, I'm going to do this dang thing, and nothing's going to stop me.* I'm taking matters in my own hands. I know there's a way, I just have to find it. So many people get discouraged and quit right away. Please don't, do it for you. Say to yourself, what if I can, what if I make it? How will that feel? How proud of myself will I be? I can wave at all the haters.... if that's not motivation, I don't know what is.

Running a contracting business can get hectic, crazy, stress-ful, but fun at the same time. I enjoy a good challenge, and my company gives me that daily. There are so many stories that I could tell just from my experience in the contracting business. I'll explain a day in the life of a contractor who knows how to take so-called problems and turn them into solutions. My brain is wired a little differently, and I know this because I listen to people talk every day, and usually, I hear *You can't do that* or *That won't work,* and I usually don't say much and just get it done. Then I get to enjoy the look on people's faces when I make it happen. In business you have to be able to think on the fly, improvise, make the customer smile and feel comfortable. You have to make things happen when no one else knows how to. People lean on you for answers all day every day. I consist-ently problem solve... it's part of the gig. If you have a business or run things at work, you may not even have a high position, but people still rely on you because you come up with the an-swers. Whatever it may be, if you want to lead you to have to be able to get it done!

For instance, we were doing a roof, tearing off the old and putting on the new. It gets messy at times, and once in a while the neighbors get agitated. It's a loud job. We had a few of our things on the neighbor's lawn, and he started yelling at a worker, and at the same time, we ran out of gas for the compressor. As I was walking over to talk to the screaming neighbor, one of my guys said that his roofing gun broke, it was missing a screw. I told him I would deal with it in a minute. I introduced myself to the neighbor. I said, "Hi, my name is Matt, and I'm running the job site. What seems to be the problem?" He started raising his voice to me, and I said, "Sorry, what was your name?" He said, "I'm Jim - now get your stuff off my lawn!" I said, "Hey Jim no problem I'll get right on it!" I added, "I noticed your roof looks pretty new; when did you get it done?" He said two years ago. I said, "Oh ok it looks good, they did a fine job," which they did. I asked, "How long have you lived here?" He told me fifteen years. I said, "It's a nice neighborhood. I can tell you keep up with your house." He said, "Yeah, it is a nice neighborhood!" He then started to become civil and said, "Yeah, I know you're just doing your job, but I would appreciate it if you tried to stay off my lawn." I said, "You're completely right. I'm going to personally make sure we do a great job of picking up, no worries. Here is my card with my cell number on it. Call me if you need anything."

Things happen when you're running a job, sometimes back to back problems or situations occur, and you have to stay ready, be on point and stay poised and in control. If you start freaking out, you're not going to have the respect of your employees, partners or customers. This happens in life as well; sometimes everything is fine then Wham! Everything hits us at once. Take a deep breath and handle one thing at a time. Don't get overwhelmed; we're only human, we can only do so much. Stay in control and stay calm. I know life gets tough, but we can always pull through, just put the effort in, keep the faith and push forward. You'll work it out in the end.

When I was around 26, I wanted to go to Europe with my good friend Tony. I had never traveled overseas, so I was going to do whatever it took to get there. I asked Tony how much money we would need to save up and he said $3,500 each. So, for a few months, I stayed home and didn't do anything. I was doing side jobs and anything I could to make money. I didn't spend money on anything. I found a way to save. I called him and said I got it. He said awesome, let's get to work. A month later we were backpacking in Europe. We went to Iceland,

Amsterdam, a few places in Italy, Milan, Venice and Vincenza, Barcelona, Berlin, and Budapest. It was pretty wild going to all those places in 12 days. By the end, I was worn out. I met some great people and had memories to last a lifetime. I found a way to do it, it wasn't easy, but I did it and had some great stories because of it. I remember telling a few people, and they had a look of disbelief, like yeah right like you're going to backpack in Europe. I sent them a postcard. Sometimes it's best to move in silence, that way there's less noise when you splash on something. All the sudden you're like pow! Here I am.

No matter what it is, something small, big, whatever, if we put our energy into finding a way instead of complaining and whining, we will be much better off. Put in the effort and dig deep. I think about Michael Jordan's flu game, which has probably been written about 1,000 times, but it was incredible. He dug deep and found a way to play. He left it all on the floor. Think about soldiers at war, what they have to go through, bullets whizzing by, their brothers getting killed in action. They do whatever is necessary to survive and to protect the men and women next to them. I respect the men and women in our military in a great way. I salute them and am very grateful for their service. Appreciation to the fullest.

I can make you an absolute promise, and that is problems will occur in your life. Things will happen that are out of your control. Leave it in GOD'S hands. GOD doesn't put you through what you can't handle. It's all about how we respond and take the bull by the horns. We have to be proactive in our response to the situation at hand. I literally problem solve from 6:00 am to the time I rest my head every day all day. When people bring me problems, my mind immediately thinks of solutions. That's a gem, take it and run with it. You have to wire your brain to problem solve. Instead of saying, gee life is so tough why me, I have the worst luck, blah, blah blah, think to yourself, how I can solve this? After a while, it's like second nature. You automatically solve things out of repetition and practice. I don't think, I just do. It comes to me naturally. It will work for you as well if you stay positive and have confidence. Over time your confidence will build up, like anything else. Practice, practice, practice. Experience comes with time, and you'll get better and better. Shine bright!

The hardest, most painful experiences that I went through in my life was losing my babies... three different times my fiancée and I had miscarriages. We all go through our hard times and turmoil, we all have times when we say why me, why did this happen? No one understands the pain but the person or people going through it. That's why it's important to treat people well because you never know what they're going through. I never talked about this; I didn't tell many people. I don't like people feeling sorry for me, and I don't like talking about something that ripped my soul in half. However, I'm speaking on it because it's possible that you can relate to a feeling of overwhelming loss, too. All I can say is there is no easy way to deal with losing a child or someone close, and I've lost them both. I got through it from the grace of GOD. I was in pain for days and mourned, but I got it together and pushed forward. I know it was even harder for Benita. I respect her strength and courage.

We also lost a family member Jimmy recently. Jimmy was the most loving person I can think of; he had such a good spirit. I know the family is in pain, but I know he's in a good place. I have his beautiful smile in my memories forever. He will always shine. Love you Jimmy.

When something happens in your life that is traumatizing, you have two choices: lay down and curl up forever or keep fighting. You have to know that there's a way you'll get through. You have to dig deep and find the inner you that is a survivor. If you're going through something now, whether you're battling an illness, you've lost a loved one, been molested, have depression, suffering from domestic mental or physical abuse, if you feel alone or weak, believe me when I tell you this – you can do it. You can fight your way out of whatever you're going through. Trust in GOD, have Faith, push forward, fight, fight, fight – don't stop fighting. There's going to be times you want to give up.... DONT don't give up, push, push, don't let go, don't give in. That's what the enemy wants, but we are made from greatness. We are strong and we can do extraordinary things when faced with adversity. Reach out to a loved one, and if you don't have anyone close you have to find the strength within. Please, I'm telling you, never stop fighting, don't give up, you can do it.

"If you can't fly, then run,
If you can't run, then walk,
If you can't walk, then crawl,
But whatever you do,
You've got to keep moving forward."
–Martin Luther King Jr.

Be Bold

I spotted a pair of Blue polo sunglasses at Macy's one day and I thought they were pretty dope, so I tried them on. I asked the saleswoman, "How do they look?" She said they look great and I said, "The only thing is, they're blue, and they don't match with everything." The saleswoman looked at me and said, "Yeah, but how 'bold' are you? If you have a boldness about you, you can wear anything." I thought *Wow! You're right. I am bold. I will take them.* Now, she could have just been telling me what I wanted to hear to get the sale, but I didn't care because she said something that made sense to me. That was five years ago, and I'm writing about it in my book today.

We can be or do anything we want in life, literally. Sometimes we have to break the rules — anything that's not off the wall. You just have to believe in yourself, have a vision and an action plan. Then have a boldness about yourself that no one can stop. I'm a very humble person. I come from a humble beginning; however, I'm confident and bold. I feel like I'm the best salesman on the planet when I'm out there selling jobs. Everyone should believe they're the best and strive for it. Boldness comes with confidence. To achieve confidence, you have to have experience; you have to roll your sleeves up and get dirty.

The more you do something, the better you get and the more confidence you obtain. Eventually, it becomes natural, but don't ever get satisfied or comfortable, that's when you get tripped up and stomped.

There's a part in the movie "Young Guns 2" when Emilio Estevez (whose character portrays Billy the Kid) is talking to his gang and says, "Every day we need to test ourselves, and once we stop testing ourselves, we get slow, and that's when they kill ya." Now I'm not saying that literally, but I do believe if we stop being hungry and having a boldness about our goals we want to achieve then we slow down, and someone else takes our spot. Jesus was Bold. Matthew 21:12 says "Jesus entered the temple courts and drove out all who were buying and selling there. He overturned the tables of money." Jesus didn't like what was going on in the place of worship, so he made a very bold statement, and people paid attention. In life there are many ways to get your point across, sometimes you got to flip a table to show some people you're not playing around.

Being bold is a lifestyle.

You have a certain power within that says *I don't care what the crowd is doing; I'm going to do what I believe is right. I'm sticking to what my gut says and rolling with it.* If someone says oh you like that person? And you like them, tell them "Absolutely, why? You have a problem with that?" Be bold in your lifestyle, your daily statements, and the way you move. I believe in being kind and treating people well, but I also believe in telling people to chill out when they are getting out of line.

Being bold can be found in all shapes sizes and colors. Being bold is for everyone. Be bold in creating things. Stop worrying about other people's opinions. Create what is really yelling at your soul. Wake up and be bold.

> *"You must do the things you think you cannot do"*
> *– Eleanor Roosevelt*

It's crucial to put out there what it is you want, what you're going after, and what is it you want to do.

If you're all over the place, you need to get organized and put together a plan. When I pray, I ask for wisdom, knowledge, and guidance in the area I'm seeking. I confess it and have faith it's going to happen. Then I come up with a specific plan of action for how to make it happen.

Write it down, write it down, write it down!!!

I have a little piece of paper that I carry in my wallet at all times with at least one goal on it. I look at it all the time. It reminds me where I need to be and what I should be doing. Anything that sways you off the path, stay clear from it. I didn't make this up or invent it. I learned from the greats and created my own style. Listen! The other day I opened an old goal composition book from 6 years ago. I don't even remember writing everything in there. But everything I wrote I now have. It blew my mind. I was thrown back a bit to tell you the truth. GOD is so good I'm truly blessed for everything I have.

I will give you an example. Let's say you want to make $75,000 a year and you're currently making $50,000. Well, you have to write this: "I __ (say your name here) ___will make $75,000 in 20__ (whatever year you pick) I am going to do this by making money where I'm at or start a side hustle."

So, you need to increase your income by $25,000. How can you do it? There are many ways – you may be able to make more sales where you currently are and so you may have to study. Study the highest paid salesman/saleswoman where you are. Study books, YouTube videos, everything you can get your hands on. A lot of information is free. Go to seminars! You have to try and make more where you're at. If that doesn't work, start a side gig/side hustle/side business... whatever you want to call it. If you're hungry and creative, you'll find a way. If you knock on 20 doors and say, "Hi my name is _ (say your name here) ___ is there anything I can help you with? I'm trying to make a few dollars." Someone will say yes. Then you say, "Is there anyone else you know who could use some help?" So, on and so forth.

Which brings me to another angle of asking: you have to be willing to open your mouth and ask. I've offered thousands of people to measure their roof. As you know, my partner and I went door to door for two years straight. It wasn't fun, but boy did I learn a lot. I got used to getting denied and grew thick skin. Rejection does not affect me. I kiss rejection. Now I'm at a point in my life where I'm asking millionaires if they want to invest in me for business purposes. My confidence is there, and I'm willing to ask. If they say no, I'll thank them and ask again a year later. People get so scared to ask for things. The worst that could happen is they say no. Oh well, at least you tried. I'm the type of person who can't sleep if I don't take a shot, I need to know where I stand. When asking for money or an opportunity, people want to know you're legit. So, it's very important that you build up your reputation and represent it right. Don't play any games, be honest and have great communication skills. The investor has to feel comfortable and know they'll get their investment back. Don't waste anybody's time.

"There are people that sit there and plan, and plan, and plan, and never do anything, and there are those who step out and take action. The world rewards those who take action"
—Bob Proctor

Excuses Are Weak

E xcuses are weak! When people come at me with excuses, it's hard for me to relate. Yes, I understand I need
to have compassion, an open heart, empathy, and be
helpful. However, I'm built differently. When I mess up, I own
it. And believe me, I've messed up plenty of times in my life. I
just own it. I accept responsibility and eat it. It's hard for me
even to spew out an excuse; excuses are weak, and I want no
part of them.

I've owned a business for ten years, and I've never missed a
day of work, so I'm not exactly the right person to tell excuses
to. Some people live their lives giving excuses daily. If that's
you, I suggest you train your mind to be stronger and switch
your mindset. Start listening to positive motivational audios,
videos, and books. If you're someone who's always late, get up
earlier, set 4 alarms, do what you've got to do, don't be weak.
When I open my eyes in the morning, I'm ready to grind, I got
a fire in me. I've had people work for me that come in late, and
they think nothing of it.

When people are late for work it drives me nuts, it shows me
that you're irresponsible and I can't trust you with a higher

position. The highest-level people are early every day, and they're the best at their craft.

When I was 19 years old, I worked for a very successful business owner named Keith, who is now a good friend of mine. I was supposed to be at work at 8 am; I clocked in at 8:01. Keith flipped out on me! He said, "If you start at 8:00, you should be clocked in at 7:50 or before." I accepted it and said, "Ok, it wouldn't happen again." I knew he was right. He was, about his business and now so am I. Time is something you can never get back. If you're a business owner and someone is late 15 minutes every day, five days a week, that's 75 minutes that could have helped the business. It distracts the workflow, it's a burden for others to pick up the slack, and it gives me grey hair.

Some people are just lazy and don't care, but to be honest, these are the people that won't excel or ever reach their full potential. Yeah, it's a bold statement, but it's the truth. I always respect the people who are honest with me and lay it down how it is. I don't want to hear lies or sugar-coated excuses. Just tell me the truth, we'll figure it out and move on. I don't get caught up in feelings. Gary Vaynerchuk said, "There's no room for emotions in the big leagues." Feelings can get you killed. When I first started my business, I used to entertain gossip, meaning I would listen and then respond with fire. It was a tough year for me because I let emotions get to me.

I would think to myself, *Dang I just helped him put food on his table,* or *I just helped pay his gas bill,* or *wow I just helped him get a car,* on and on and on. People would talk behind my back, and back then I let it get to me. Now, if people come to me with gossip I say, "I tell ya what, I don't care and if it's not going to build up my company in a good way – save it for someone else." To own a construction company you have to have thick skin.

Thick! Now, I let things bounce off me, and they don't influence me like before. Sure, you can get bothered but let it bounce off and keep it moving. I realized feelings are weak when it comes to gossip. When you're doing great things and making money and shining, there will be haters. You have to push forward and not care about other people's opinions. If you're doing the right things, treating people well, you'll be fine.

I've become bolder as I've gotten older. I know it can be hard for some people to handle. I don't know how else to tell it sometimes. I'm very careful with my words because I believe a true man of GOD should always try and uplift people, not bring them down. However, sometimes you have to be straightforward with people. And some people may not like my technique, but I know eventually they will realize – hopefully - that I was just being sincere and honest. I've had people close to me give me constructive criticism before, and I took it well, and I made corrections in my life. It's important not to just hang with yes men and people who love everything you do. You need a few people to tell you the truth, especially if you're off track.

I wrote this book the way I wanted to write it. I didn't ask anyone's opinion or advice as far as content. Everything I'm writing is 100% from my mind. My knowledge comes from studying great people and my own life's experiences. I didn't research how to write or worry about certain guidelines; I'm doing it my way. There are words I use that may not be grammatically correct, but that's ok, I choose to use specific words, this way people can really feel the way my mind thinks and works. I want everyone to understand my way of life and philosophies. If you believe in something and put forth your best effort, then there's nothing to worry about. You let your heart show, and the rest is in GOD's hands. I believe I will help millions of people with this book! That's the prayer.

I believe if I can help people create a better, more positive mindset for themselves, they will live a better life. Everything I've been studying and learning for the last ten years I project in my own views and language and I pray it helps people. If you enjoy this book and feel it can help people, it would mean the world to me if you spread the word about it.

Mindset:
Bulletproof Mentality

Most people are probably familiar with the words mindset and mentality. It all starts with how you maintain and feed your mind. If we have a positive mindset life is much more enjoyable. Some people keep their focus on bad news, gossip, and things that have negative energy. I have no idea how people can indulge in so much chaos. It's good to be up to date with the news and being informed, but if all you're doing is arguing and getting mad at people for their opinions, then you should check yourself. Just because my opinion is different than yours doesn't make me right, or you wrong. If we spent more time focused on positive things and less on the negative, we would live a more uplifting life. Before we go to bed, we should be thinking about dreams, goals, our action plans to success, not thinking and talking about the latest gossip on TV or negative information. Its ok to unwind for an hour, but too much negativity is not good for the soul. Balance and moderation are soul food. Limit the negativity you're feeding your mind.

There are all types of mindsets that call for different situations. When you're lifting weights, you probably want to go into beast mode and get hyped up. Or when you're running, you might want to throw on some music that gets you going. When I was waking up at 4:30 am to work out, I would put on motivational YouTube videos. To each his own. Different times call for different measures. When you're with kids, you want to get in teacher mode, fun mode, helpful mode.

In my business, I have to be stern and mean what I say, or I would get rolled over in a heartbeat. I'm a kind person, but people will take you out if they know you're a pushover. Your character gets exposed if you're weak. We recently did a handful of roofs in 90-degree weather. It's 10 degrees hotter on the roof, if not more. If you're not mentally prepared, then you won't make it. Plus, you have to wear the right gear and drink massive amounts of water. Some people just can't make it; it's not an easy trade. If you've ever worked in the heat then you know that your body reacts differently, it doesn't move as fast. The sun sucks all your energy from you, so if you're not ready for the heat then get out of the kitchen. It takes a warrior mindset to do a roof in the 90-100-degree weather. Shout out to all the roofers getting it in.

When I was in my young 20's, I had the wrong mindset. I was getting in a lot of fights and altercations because I thought I was The Man. Well, I wasn't. I got arrested a few times and spent the night in the Holding Center. The longest I ever been in jail was two days and let me tell you that was long enough for me to realize I was a dummy. I was doing things and putting myself in the wrong situations. I was sitting there in the holding center behind bars by myself. I got in a fight downtown over something stupid, and now I was paying the consequences. I thought I was going to be able to leave the next day, but I had to stay for two days. My shirt was all ripped, I had dried blood on me, and I knew I made a mistake. When you're sitting there, you have nothing but time to reflect on where you are in life and what you need to do. I said to myself *What you are doing? Is this what you want to do with your life?* I was asking myself these types of questions. I realized then that I had to get myself together, watch the partying and stop putting myself in the wrong places with the wrong people.

I also learned the hard way that I wasn't indestructible. I got in a fight a different time, well I got jumped and got my butt kicked, which was a good thing for my mindset. I still have a thick scar on my head; it's a good reminder to stay humble. I was a little too aggressive and needed to calm down. I think we all need a good butt whooping one time in our life if we are getting out of control. I'm very humble and stay clear of bad vibes and negative situations. I knew I had to get on track and put myself in the right situations and stay out of the nightlife. At that point, I slowly started to move differently, and my eyes opened more, and I started to look around.

If you find yourself getting in trouble, getting locked up, getting in fights, **it's probably your fault.** I know a lot of people who say that trouble follows them. That's a bunch of bull. Accept the responsibility, accept the fact that you need to make some changes. I know I did. If you're getting caught up in drama, arguments or whatever it may be, you have to start with yourself and analyze who you're around. Maybe it's you, and you have to make some changes, maybe it's the people around you, and you have to cut some people off. You have to elevate your mindset put yourself in better situations. Watch what you're putting in your body, whatever it is that's holding you back. It's time for us to take charge and shoot for the mountain-top. Let's be great as people, let's progress and shine bright. I know it's hard and circumstances may not be easy for you, believe me, I feel you. I had to dig my way out little by little, and it took years. But I dug in, and never looked back. There is no room for giving up, that is not an option. Push through, break the doors down, rip the hinges off. Have a mindset that is fearless. Believe in yourself, have faith, confess it and put things into action.

A military mindset is a lot more intense, and your life depends on it. It's not a game, and only a small percentage can make it. My cousin told me many stories of when he was fighting in the war in Iraq and Afghanistan. War is incomprehensible to someone who wasn't in the trenches. I never served, although I tried. I have high blood pressure, so, unfortunately, they wouldn't allow me to join the Army. I know the stories and watched documentaries, but I will never truly understand what they have been through. I have the utmost respect for the Men and Women who serve in the military. I don't take their sacrifice lightly and am very grateful for their commitment. Thank you!

My cousin is a great leader. I've learned many great attributes and strengths from him on leadership and mindset. I remember one evening going in his room, unannounced, haha! He probably still won't know I was reading all his stuff until he reads this book. I was reading all of his awards, achievements, and medals. It was very impressive, and I am proud to be related to such an honorable Soldier and leader.

Here's a story my cousin told me that stood out about mindset. There are different degrees: there's a mindset of having a good day, and then there's a mindset of survival. The scale is very wide. It's up to us to adjust and adapt to situations. If you ever get stuck in the desert or on an island, your instincts better kick in, or you'll be just an empty memory. Yeah, it's harsh, but if you're soft and get pushed to the limit, you might not make it, and it all starts in the mind.

They called it Bloody January, the year was 2004 in Baqubah, Iraq which is 50km to the northeast of Bagdad. It was one of the most dangerous places on earth at the time. That's where my cousin was. He was in the Infantry. It was a really stressful time over there. There were a lot of casualties from mortars, rocket fire, and roadside bombs. They just took over the mayor's complex and everyone wanted them dead. Twenty soldiers and Marines were holding down that area. A new Major came in at that point with a new group of soldiers and Marines. Some of the new group coming in were young. The Major and the new team were gearing up to go out and although my cousin didn't agree with them going out at that particular time, it was irrelevant because he was outranked. The roads were 'blacked out', which means filled with roadside bombs. He knew if they went out there, his team would have to follow to help out. The new Major and his team went out, and not even a ½ mile down the road they got hit.

My cousin's team had to go out and help bring them back. It was a chaotic time. There were casualties and injuries. When they got back, my cousin was getting the vehicles together and trying to make sense of everything. He was cleaning blood out of the Humvee, and that's when it really hit him. The anger, sadness, and frustration had to be tough to deal with. There was a lot happening fast, and he knew he had to do something.

The morale was beaten up. My cousin asked himself "How do I hold it together? How do I keep my team alive? How can I be the most effective?" These were all the things going through my cousin's head. He knew he had to do something; pep talks didn't work anymore, inspirational speeches were over. Nothing was working. Survival mode kicked in his mind. He was praying for an hour straight daily, looking for answers. Real faith was in the atmosphere. He said when bullets are whizzing by your head, people get religious really quick. There was only one way to survive; it was to get his team to have a "No Fear, Bulletproof" mentality. He said he had to fake his bravery, which isn't really faking because we all know you sometimes have to trick or fake yourself into doing things or becoming what you believe you can become to survive. **Fake courage becomes real courage in the face of adversity.** He said he built up his team to be cocky, bulletproof and to believe they had the armor of GOD. There was no other way to survive. Nothing else worked, so they became what the atmosphere called for. They were all highly trained, but it was the mindset that set them apart, nothing could stop them. Embrace the pain and the suck. Mind over matter. If it's cold, the cold will go away... when you're going through hell, keep pushing through because there's another side. After they developed their "Bulletproof Mentality" their morale was up, and they demonstrated an invincible attitude. From there on out, it was a different attitude, and no one got in their way. Missions were more stable; the enemy started to fear them more and more because of their fearless presence.

Was everything perfect? Absolutely not, but the mentality was fearless. If my cousin had let the cleaning of the blood affect his mind, and the loss of life and injuries crumble him, more lives would have been lost. He had no choice but to be fearless and spread that belief and mindset. He had to find a way to dig deep and pull out the most extreme mental state known to man.

He is a true soldier, a true leader, and I salute him, his team, and the military for their sacrifice for our freedom. I know I speak for all of us when I say we are forever indebted for the sacrifice and service they give to the United States of America. Thank you.

This is the most extreme case of bulletproof mentality. I shared this because some of us complain because it's hot or cold or we get mad because our plane got delayed. Stop being so weak. We have men and women who died for our flag and our freedom. Imagine your son or daughter going out in a war with roadside bombs and the enemy trying to take their head off any chance they got. We sit in our air-conditioned office complaining on Facebook about our girlfriend or boyfriend not paying enough attention to us or get mad because our boss doesn't treat us fairly. We need to be stronger. Fake your mentality until it becomes real. Take on anything that comes your way, stop complaining and start dominating your time here on Earth. It all starts with the mind. So, when you do something, do it with a "Bulletproof Mentality".

Fear is an illusion, it's not real unless we give it power. Now I'm not saying getting chased by a bear in the woods is an illusion, but the fear of certain things like: starting a business, fear of our kids getting hurt, fear of losing our job, fear of sickness, fear of a break up, whatever your fear is don't give it energy, don't give it power. If you feed into it your fear, you're helping it grow. You may make your fear a reality. A lot of things are out of our hands, we can only control so much. Being a responsible parent involves putting your family in the safest position, but you can't control all the variables. We need to leave it in GOD's hands and do our best. Take it as it comes. I think we get scared as humans of failing or people judging us. Man, forget that, who gives a dang about their opinions? Just be yourself.

I had a restaurant business once that didn't do so well, and the feedback from many people was that of, "Oh I'm so sorry it didn't work out." But my thought was, "Oh well, at least I tried and didn't sit on my butt and say what if?" I love taking chances. I love jumping in, if it doesn't work out oh well. Pick up what's left and keep it moving. Sorry to tell you this but not everything is going to work out just right. Stop being afraid to take a chance. We always regret the chances we don't take. I tell people that are worried about starting a business, "What's the worst that could happen?" We talk about the worst thing and the worst thing usually isn't that bad. Then they say, *You know what, it isn't that scary.* It's good to have an attitude of no failure, but it's also good to have a backup plan. Being prepared is intelligent.

So, when you head out of the house for the day, be prepared for this crazy world. Stay prayed up. If we fall in the trap of letting negative people ruin are day, we're not ready for battle. Let's face it, just living as a human being on a regular day basis is hard enough. When you throw in other factors, it gets complicated. It's all good though., as long as we are ready, and if we are mentally prepared for combat. There's going to be haters, opposition, and people that want us to fail and get mad when we shine. I smile and wave. I won't allow anyone to steal my joy. Yeah, I may get frustrated, but then I talk to myself and say *Listen self, you are great, you are strong, and you will not allow anyone to take you off course.*

Have a Bulletproof Mentality, no fear, stay hungry, stay blessed, be grateful, know that everything is going to be ok. Have faith in yourself and push through. Your mind is extremely powerful. You can do anything. Sometimes I smile at every single person I encounter, especially when I'm in a funky mood, I trick myself into happiness. It works, I'm telling you. Try it. Sometimes you have to trick yourself to get to the next level. Mindset is where it starts, so I hope you have a beautiful day and stay driven.

Show Up

How do the greatest performers, musicians, athletes, speakers, preachers, teachers, writers, waitresses, waiters, bartenders, dancers, comedians, roofers, carpenters, doctors, lawyers, nurses, gymnasts, entrepreneurs, and everybody else become the best in their field? They show up! They practice consistency and put in the work. Do you think Floyd Mayweather became one of the greatest boxers by going to the gym twice a week? Absolutely not. He consistently worked harder than the next man. He has never lost a fight, he's 50-0. He goes above and beyond. He went the extra mile. He put in more than the next man.

Most importantly, he showed up. People can hate and argue about him, but it doesn't matter, the record speaks for itself. How did Serena Williams become so dominant? She has been putting in that work since she was a child. She started when she was 3. Serena won 23 Titles and has accomplished so much in her young life. She is amazing. She didn't get there from practicing once a week, she went all in, and got busy every day. She says she hates working out but does it to maintain her health and keep her from injury. She also knows, to be the best you need to work harder than your opponent. When you're a champion, you show up every day, and when you don't want to run, you run anyway.

I don't know why they created the snooze button. It should be called the lazy button. When you hear that sound to wake up you should be ready to conquer the day. Honestly, I rarely get woken up by my alarm. I'm usually awake 15 minutes before it goes off. I know we are all different, but having some fire helps especially to start the day. I knocked on doors for two years straight, my partner and I didn't take days off. While my friends were at the beach partying, I was in my khakis with my shirt tucked in asking if I could measure their roof or if they needed anything done. As I have said, I learned a lot about rejection, and I ate it up like a champ. We showed up every day and played the numbers game. We knew if we asked enough people, we could eventually get work. Two years of that wasn't fun, but I did it with dedication and created a successful business.

I was laying in my hotel bed in Montego Bay, Jamaica. I was on vacation with my friend Sam Dizzle. It was an all-inclusive resort which means you can eat as much as you want, and I did. We had a great relaxing time, but I felt groggy and unhealthy. I started getting chest pains because I was overeating. I wasn't taking good care of myself at that time. I said a prayer and knew I had to make some changes. I asked GOD to let me get back home alive. I have a 5-year-old son and a family to take care of. When I got back home, I stuck with my decision. I joined a 6-week challenge to lose 20 pounds. It was a $600 investment, but if you lose the weight you get your money back. If not, you're out the money. It was a workout program Monday through Friday. The only time I could do it was early. So, I signed up for 5:30 am every day. They gave me a meal plan. No pop, (I'm from Buffalo, NY, so I call it pop, you may call it soda), no alcohol, only black coffee, no carbs, no sweets, and the workout program. I gave up a lot at once. I would eat six times a day and could replace a meal with a shake. I ate a lot of chicken, broccoli, and fruit. 4oz of chicken, steamed broccoli and fruit was my go to meal. Also, a gallon of water a day. That's hard to drink every day. If you never tried, give it a try, it's not that easy. I would wake up every morning at 4:30 a.m. say my prayers for the day, eat a small piece of fruit and start my early journey. When I did this, it was in the middle of winter. I would have to scrape the ice and snow off my car before I could even leave my driveway, and then be on my way to the gym.

Just to backtrack a bit, let me explain a little psychology that I learned along the way. The first thing my mind would say to me is *Lay back down, sleep in, you can miss one time.* I immediately shut those thoughts down and prayed for strength. Then on the way to the gym, I would listen to Eric Thomas and other motivational speakers on YouTube to get in the right state of mind. If you're not familiar with him, he's a motivational speaker. All you have to do is go to YouTube and type in motivational videos and thousands pop up. It's a good thing to get you going and light your fire. I also love to listen to David Goggins; he's extraordinary. I know we are all different when it comes to motivation. I probably could have still done it without the motivation, but it amps me up even more and makes me feel like I'm a beast, which I am. At 5 am when I was driving, there was barely anybody on the road. I was pretty much the only one out there doing what I do, which is to dominate. I felt at one; I was at peace. Every morning I was usually the first one there. I would work out, then come home, eat two eggs, shower and take my son to school. It was a 6-week ritual. It was very challenging for me, but I conquered the mind, that was the hard part. The physical part was easy for me. I would tell myself *Get up and show up, make it there.* I ended up losing 25 pounds and 6.7% body fat. I was happy and felt good. As long as you're showing up consistently, you will see results. Grind baby, grind!

It all starts with a decision. You have to say ok; I'm ready to do this, whatever that may be. Then show up day in and day out. Don't let anyone talk you out of what you set out to do. Don't let the negative thoughts in. When they come in (and believe me they will) you have to replace them with good thoughts, strong thoughts, positive thoughts. Put something on that inspires you or listen or read something that gets you where you need to be. When the mind is where it needs to be, take immediate action.

Show up, show up, show up!

Showing up can be for anything. It can be learning how to play an instrument, flying a plane, starting a business, learning how to dance, act, sing, anything. The important thing is you go all out, don't half step. Put your entire heart into your goals. There are exceptions of course. Like maybe you just always wanted to try something, so you do it for a little bit so that you knew how it was or felt. You want to get a taste. I did this with Brazilian Jiu-Jitsu. I went for a few weeks to learn some basics. It's a whole other lifestyle and amazing art for those people who practice it daily; I have the utmost respect for them. It's a lot of mental and practice. I loved it. I got my butt kicked for a few weeks just because I wanted to taste it. It was a hell of an experience.

When I played basketball, it was my life. I played every day, all day. I would always play with the bigger kids, so I got better and wasn't intimidated when I got to organized basketball. I would practice on my dribbling, shooting and everything else all the time. My friends and I would go from court to court playing anyone and everyone. The reason I had success is because of how much work I put in. I never played college ball, because I ended up with a knee injury, but I was pretty good in my sophomore, junior and senior years. I racked up some trophies. I'm not saying I was incredible or that I was getting scouted, but I was a hustler. The reason why I did well was all those years of dedicated practice. We used to shovel the snow so that we could play in the winter – true story! I would go to intramurals before school started. Even then, I had to earn my spot. In 7th grade, I wrestled so my wrestling coach wasn't happy I chose to play basketball the next year. He ran basketball in the morning and would bust my chops, but I was determined to be good. Another reason I excelled was because of my work ethic and persistence. A group of friends and I played consistently every day without fail; it was the love for the game. I miss those days playing ball. I showed up to play every day and had fun doing it.

I was inspired by Coach Gross to write the chapter "Find a Way" for this book. He was a father figure to me. Up to that point, it was the hardest I had ever been pushed. I loved it. I love when someone gets the best out of me. I remember him bringing me in his office and saying, "Listen; I want you to dominate, I want you to score more, I want you to take control out there." Hearing that from a coach is awesome. I said, "So you want me to shoot more and score more?" and he said, "Yes!" In my mind, I was thinking, *Man I just got a free pass to score, this is great!* My boy Joe and I used to have incredible chemistry on the court, and some guys would get mad because we always had the ball, but hey I did what the coach asked.

If you're going to college and you're missing classes, you better get it together. Don't waste your time or money. If you hate it and don't show up, why are you there anyway? If your goal is to learn the guitar, why are you missing your classes? Either show up and practice or stop lying to yourself. Excuses are weak. Whatever it is, wherever you are in your life, just go for it and have fun doing it! Life is good – smile.

If you love to read or write books, good for you – that is an amazing gift, and I'm happy for you. You should help others get to your level. I read a book called the "Slight Edge" by Jeff Olson. My friend recommended it to me for which I'm grateful. I love it when people tell me about books. That's how I've come across a lot of great ones. Or usually authors will recommend books they read, and you start digging. Back to "Slight Edge", this book explains how to break down things little by little, to chip away at things. It recommends reading something like ten pages a day. If you do that you could bust out a book in three weeks or less. That's like 15-20 books a year. Imagine how much you can learn in that time, it's incredible.

That's how I started to write my book. I would write notes and ideas and put it down on my computer each day. Then I sat down with a great man of GOD, his name is Nathan Salter, and he has written many great books. He gave me clarity and direction which helped tremendously. I knew I had to write, so I started with a small goal of writing 400 words a day. I blew that out the water and realized writing thousands of words a day was within my grasp. I pick up on a lot of what people say, so when someone drops a gem, I soak it up. I was listening to a Joe Rogan motivational YouTube video, and he was talking about getting work done. He said when you don't feel like writing, do it anyway and the next thing you know you'll have 1,000 words. So, I now make my goal at least 1,000 a day. He's someone who did it, he's already successful so why wouldn't I emulate the work ethic of a man who is very talented and successful?

I show up every day at this computer and get it in. I trained myself. People get to caught up in being perfect. People need to stop planning so much and start doing. Talk is cheap; action is everything. My goal for writing this book is to inspire people to progress and move forward. To stay uplifted and believe in themselves. We beat ourselves up too much. I know I used to myself and it's unhealthy. I want people to push themselves to the maximum. We have to test ourselves; we have to try new things and not be scared of failure. Forget people's opinion about you. Just do what you've got to do and be a lion. If I had listened to everyone's opinion, I wouldn't be where I am today. People will try and tear your dreams apart because they are jealous sometimes and can't do what you do. If you sniff out hate around you, you should watch what you say around them and don't share your next move. It's sad, but you have to move in silence, it's the best way. Next thing you know you drop something hot and everyone is like "Whaaatttttt?"

I'm writing this book, and I'm exhausted because we did a huge roof today on a bank. It was really hot working in the sun all day – it's draining. My eyes are heavy, and I feel like laying down. But I choose to press forward, I choose to break through and show up on this laptop and put my thoughts together. I'm so focused on this book that nothing is going to stop me. If I go lay down, it will drive me nuts, so why not get some work done? I know this book needs to be in people's hands. I know I'm going to help people, so I'm determined to get it done. Every single day I show up and start writing, re-writing, editing notes, coming up with new ideas, and add-ons. There are distractions, this, that, whatever; I don't care. I'm going to plug away and get as much as possible done today. Last night, I was up grinding until 3:15 A.M., I went to bed and woke up at 6:00 A.M. and was on top of a roof by 7:00 A.M. I learned to have the drop on everyone else, to be at the top of the food chain you have to sleep less, party less, and grind and hustle more. Show up day in and day out and stay ready.

Les Brown tells a story about the Chinese bamboo tree. A man took very well care of his bamboo tree, watered it and cared for it, but everyone thought he was crazy because they couldn't see anything coming out of the ground. This went on for five years. The people laughed and made fun of him because they didn't see any results. Well, that 5th year, the Chinese bamboo tree shot up 80 feet in the air, and everyone was shocked. Most people would have given up, but the man knew he was nurturing that tree and it would eventually grow. Sometimes in life we work towards something and don't see results fast enough, so we quit or stop right when the fruits of our labor are ready to harvest. Success is a slow grind; you have to show up and be willing to put in the work day in and day out.

Also, with relationships, you have to put in love to see results. Everyone expects results at lightning speed! We want it, and we want it right now. The man taking care of the tree didn't listen to the negative talk or get discouraged. Imagine if he let the haters talk him out of caring and watering the bamboo tree. It would have never have shot up 80 feet. We have to believe in what we're doing and not let anyone discourage us. Focus on what's in front of us and have faith it's going to work out. Showing up every day is the key that gets overlooked. I've been around people who go through the motions, there's barely any effort, and their work ethic speaks for itself. Clock in, clock out.

When someone doesn't want to be there and is moping around, it's a sad sight to see. If you're going to do something, do it with energy, be enthusiastic. Some might say, "Yeah, but my job sucks..." Well, quit and do something else. Why waste your time and your employer's time? If you're in a relationship and there's no effort and you're miserable, then either go all out to fix it or keep it moving. Now, if you're married, it's different, I believe we should do everything we can to try and rebuild what you have. Work on building a relationship with balance. You both have to put in the work to make it right. Whether it's a relationship or career, business or whatever, show up day in, and day out. If you're putting in the work and doing it with love, your results should be sweet.

So, to break it down, I believe showing up is the most important thing you can do. It's based on action. Showing up and taking action are brother and sister. There comes a point when you've got to make it happen. Enough planning, listening, studying, and learning... now let's jump in and get it done. With almost everything I can think of, you learn as you go. It's not like you wake up and start speaking French. You have to learn, fall down, get some scrapes, bruises, get embarrassed, all that good stuff. Through continuous action, you will get better. You need to be there to elevate and progress. Show up and put in that work.

It's Not Too Late

A lot of times we wake up and say to ourselves, I'm not where I want to be or Am I really X years old? Where did the time go? Why didn't I try that, why didn't I start that business, why didn't I learn to play the piano? and I wish I would have traveled more... It's ok, I'm here to tell you it's not too late, there's still more time.

> *"Never Give up on a dream just because the time it will take to accomplish it. The time will pass anyway"*
> *–Earl Nightingale*

Ask yourself, why not start the business, why not learn the piano, why not travel, why not do whatever it is you always wanted to do? I'm telling you right now – if you are discouraged, scared or timid, pull your bootstraps up, put your boxing gloves on, whatever it is that gets you ready and go in. Nothing can stop you, but you. You're full of greatness. Now break through, go for it and stop making excuses. There's no way I'm as far as I want to be financially in life, but I refuse to quit, I refuse to stop trying, I refuse to make up some poor excuse not to keep going. If you feel like you're too old, or it's too late, don't let that discourage you. Here's an example of some people that started late in their life who became very successful.

- ✓ Vera Wang broke into the fashion industry at the age of 40. She's now a women's award-winning premier designer. Her net worth is 650 million dollars.

- ✓ Rodney Dangerfield was 46 when he caught his first real break on the Ed Sullivan show, then went on to make some hilarious films. His net worth was around 10 million dollars.   .

- ✓ Ray Kroc was 52 when he started working for McDonald's. He was estimated to have a net worth of 500 million dollars.

- ✓ Colonel Harland Sanders, the man behind KFC, didn't come into his own until the age of 66. In 1964 he sold the franchise for 2 million dollars.

These are just a few people that started their careers later in life. I've read of people in their 70's, 80's and even 90's that started late. I encourage you to look into the full background of these people and many more. Life is not all about money; it's really about happiness within. When we are happy with ourselves, life seems to be so much more enjoyable. I'm just giving some examples of people who got a late start and became very successful. Real success is doing what you love, and if you can make a career out of it, even better. If you're an insurance agent and want to expand on the insurance you sell, then take more classes, do what's necessary to get qualified. Don't wait, sign up today. If you always wanted to make funny videos start now. Make videos every day, show them to friends and family, and the ones that they laugh at most, put those on YouTube, Facebook all the social media platforms. Get started and create.

We get stuck and start believing other people and negative people or even listening to yourself.... Stop. There is no reason not to get started. Don't put off until tomorrow what can get done today. Guess what, you'll feel better, and at least you'll know the outcome. It's never too late, get inspired, do what you always wanted to do. There's also a flip side if you're young and people say you're too young to do that, don't listen to them, and do it anyway. When I started my business, so many people said, "Aren't you too young to own your own business?" It was a hurdle I had to climb, but I got over it and did it anyway. Nothing can stop you when you have fire and the will to succeed. When your age pops in your mind, just tell yourself, others have done it before me, and I can do it too. It's never too late; we can do incredible things when we believe in ourselves. If you're out of shape, hire a trainer or start by walking, it's not too late to get in shape. Have faith. Don't listen to the background noise, push forward; I know you can.

Business Philosophy

R eady, set, go! Action required. Now I don't claim to be a guru or the best out there, but I'm pretty dang good. I've sold thousands of deals. I know how to sell, and I know how to make people comfortable. If people are going to write you a check for $12,000 or whatever it may be, you better believe they should like you. If you come off too aggressive, impolite, or arrogant, you probably won't get the sale.

There are many ways to start a business. I'm going to give you some ideas and direction on how to get started in my fashion. These aren't exactly technical ways of starting a business, but more of philosophies and the way I did it. I've had a successful contracting business for ten years now and have investments in other businesses. I do well for myself, but it wasn't easy to get started. I've also been involved in businesses that have failed. To me it was a learning experience, so I enjoyed the process. You better know a decent amount about the business you get started in. At least enough to be able to answer a lot of questions. Sometimes you'll have to wing it.

Believe me when I tell you I learned as I went in my business. Just make sure you're passionate and not wasting your time or anyone else's. Have a solid foundation of the groundwork you're about to engage in. The most important thing about business is your customer. You have to do a great job accommodating them and do an amazing job at taking care of their needs, otherwise, why are you in business? Know your value and what you're bringing to the table. Once you know the basics, jump! I dove in head first and never looked back. I never said to myself what if it doesn't work, because I always knew it would. I went all in and deflected all the naysayers and haters around me. So many people took it as a joke, but I didn't care. You must be able to dodge the hate and push through. It gives me fire and more of a reason to push forward.

In my business, I'm face to face with my clients, so I have to sell myself. Here are some pointers:

Look decent. Nobody wants to hand over money to someone who dresses like a slob. Each business is different; for instance, I've done estimates in a hoodie with my logo on it, jeans and sneakers. But I tell the customer before I come. I'll say, "I'm on a job site, I will come straight over and give you an estimate." And when I show up, I'll say, "Please excuse the attire, I just came from a job site." However, I like to usually wear a Polo shirt and nice jeans. I always wear clean socks. A lot of times you'll be going in their house and they don't want to see your big toe popping out of a hole. It's funny but true; you could lose a job like that. Have a mint ready, you'll be talking up close, so you don't want your breath to be kicking. Try to be decent looking that's all I'm saying. And be sure to wear business attire if you're going for that type of job.

Be on time. Punctuality is crucial. I can't harp on this enough. I'd rather be an hour early than a minute late. People are busy and have set times for everything. If you are running late, then have the courtesy to call and let them know. Your half-hour tardiness could cost you the job.

Be confident. Walk into that estimate or meeting knowing you're going to land it, get the client or the sale. Have good energy and smile. If I'm not in a great mood, then I force myself to smile. Life is too short to be mad. Try to laugh, joke, give compliments, chit-chat and find something in common if possible.

Be personable. If they have red roses in the front lawn, say, "I love your roses." Be honest, but find something about their wardrobe or house that you like and express it. It breaks the ice and shows you have not only interest in the sale but also the person. You have to connect with customers and people. I've had estimates from companies that were so disconnected that I would never give them the business. If I knew someone was trying, I would respect that more.

Respect their time. You don't want to take too much of people's time. Try and be quick but informative. Now, this doesn't happen all the time, but I've had people cook for me, make me cookies and coffee. I even went and had a beer with a married couple before. I've gone on errands with a customer, so each day brings its unique situation. Be ready for anything. It's most important to give off good energy, people look for that and can feel the vibe. Then there are some people cold as a fish, and I try and make them laugh too.

Know when to say No. This is a gem right here, don't forget it. At first, when you start, you'll want to take every client – don't. Usually, when you see a red flag, it's a red flag! Follow your gut instinct. My first year in business I took a small job that should have taken 3 hours max, and it turned into 12 hours. It was a complete nightmare, we still joke about it today. The red flag was when the guy told me he likes to be hands-on, well he was on the roof with us the whole time and made our easy job a terrible day. At one point, my brother was cutting some wood, and the customer grabbed the saw from his hands in the middle and almost cut himself. My brother put him in check, and he fell back a little after that and left us alone for a short time, a real short time. Our profit that day was minuscule. Now that I have years of experience under my belt, if this happened today, I would not allow it, I would tell him to get off the roof. I would basically say *Either let me do my job, or you can do it yourself* (of course, nicely.) Certain clients aren't worth providing a service for. No amount of money would make a difference. I told one guy I would get to him in a few weeks and he was insisting that we do the job right away. He kept calling me and bothering me. I knew what it would turn into, so I said I'm sorry I can't do the job and left it at that. Two years went by and I still see it hasn't been done. Probably no one wants to deal with him. This has only happened to me a handful of times, but it happens.

Know your worth. If someone tries to beat you up on the price, it's ok and healthy to negotiate, but don't get taken advantage of. If I give someone a price and give them my best, and they say they can't make it happen, then I say "Ok no problem if something changes give me a call, I would love to do the work for you" — a lot of times they call back. People always want a deal, and that's fine but know your limit. If you're making a phone sale or service call, the main thing is to be polite and have good energy; they can feel the energy over the phone. If you sound tired, bored and half dead, you probably won't close the deal, or the customer won't have interest. Be alive, be kind, be yourself and stand out.

Do your research. Decide what type of business you want, if it's a DBA, LLC, Corporation or Partnership. I like the LLC and Corporations because it protects you from getting sued for any business-related disputes or liabilities. If someone tries to sue you, they can only go after the business not your assets, house, cars, etc. Believe me, when you start to shine and do good, people will start to envy you and people are jealous of other's success and will try and find a way to come after you. So, protect yourself. Talk to a good lawyer for the legal advice and information needed for your particular business endeavor.

Grind. Every business is different; however, the grind is the same. If you think you're going to put in a little time here and there, you won't make it. If this is your first business and you will be counting on the income, then be ready to grind. There are no lukewarm hustlers, you either got it, or you don't. I knocked on doors for two years straight before I picked up enough momentum to start running a profitable business. Now I get most of my business from referrals. I give $200-dollar referrals to anyone who gets me a full construction job. When I do a job for someone, I always ask them to refer any friends that need any work. When I first started, there wasn't too much social media; now you can kill it on Facebook, Instagram, and a thousand other platforms. Plus, there are reviews on many different sites. People love to do their research before doing business with people. Get a professional website. Have a good name with a good color scheme and logo. People act like business cards are played out, but I still give them out every day. They are a very useful tool. Some people take a picture of it, whatever works.

Promote. You must be a walking poster board for your business. Whatever you're selling or service you're providing, you must have your eyes and ears open 24/7. When I hear someone talking about their roof my ears go up, and I say, "I'm sorry to interrupt, but did you say you needed a new roof?" I've gotten a fair number of jobs just by being on point. If you're selling hair products and hear a conversation between people and they're talking about shampoo, you better jump on it; if you don't, you'll think about it later and regret it.

Don't be scared. Being scared doesn't make money. If you want to get business in every way possible, you can't be afraid to talk to people. You don't necessarily have to try and sell something right away but plant the seed.

Don't wait. The time may never be just right! So, go for it, jump in. It's intelligent to do your research and study the game. Have a business plan and the legalities on point. Now jump! Too many people talk about it and never act. Excuses come piling in. If you're not going to do it, then stop talking about it. People don't want to hear about what you could have done. Henry Ford said, "You can't build a reputation on what you are going to do." What he means is that talk is cheap. Action and results are the truth. You're guaranteed to make mistakes, but that's part of the game.

Learn as you go. If there's someone in your field with a business, watch and soak up everything you can. Ask to work for free if necessary. This is called apprenticeship or internship and is an important step in the process of becoming successful in business for most. I learned from the guys I worked for who had their contracting company before me. I would watch, learn and repeat. You eventually come up with your own style, your niche, and then you can dominate. It doesn't happen overnight. It's a lot of work, but it's worth it. If I were going to open a coffee shop, I would go to every coffee shop in town, out of town, and around the world. I would take notes, watch videos and soak it all up. What type of cups do they use, what type of coffee bean, what creamer do they use, stir straws, outfit, greeting, color scheme, location, website, people, food, desserts, how long do they take, how much do they charge, what type of atmosphere and energy, music, what's the crowd like? It's a science, and you've got to think about every angle. However actually getting started on your mission is more important than all of that combined. None of that matters if you sit around and think about it for ten years. The people that jump in and get started are the most successful.

At one point, I opened a burger joint with two other partners. What I learned right away was it takes way longer to make a decision with three partners. You have to respect the two other people and their personalities. You also have to be open-minded to listen to other's opinions. So, it takes a lot of time for a little decision. We had great food and an awesome looking restaurant. However, it failed. Only one partner was there most of the time, the other partner and I weren't there enough. I always like to take responsibility for anything I'm involved in. I wasn't happy with the management, but in the end, I don't blame anyone but myself. I learned a ton from having that business, and now I know what not to do, and some things that I need to do better. If you're going into the restaurant business, have cameras, and go there a couple of times a day at least until it's running smooth. Trust the person running it. Make sure you count inventory and keep up with it. I was more of a silent partner, but my money wasn't silent (I lost a nice chunk). So, if I had to do it again, I would have been there more. I wouldn't take anything back; it was a learning experience. The best thing about it was I got to eat some great steak hoagies...and I love hoagies.

Be a leader. When you start a business, and you have employees, be ready to be a leader and a great listener. People will come to you for advice about the job and also advice about life. It's important that we try our best as business owners and try to help whatever the situation is. It's very important to listen and be understanding if you want to be a good leader. You have to be ready at all times to solve problems and come up with solutions very quickly. Go with your gut instincts and try not to second guess yourself. Weigh out the best-case scenario and roll with it. You'll make mistakes, just make sure you learn from them. Let people be themselves and help them excel. Communication is the key. Have fun and give out good energy.

If you're planning or thinking about starting a business, get started immediately. Start planning and get busy. Write all your ideas down, talk to a lawyer, get a name and get going. Don't tell many people about your idea because they could snatch it. Keep it in a close circle. If you have fear or doubt, don't sweat it because it's normal. Replace it with the mindset of *I know I can, I know I will,* then turn it into action and make it happen. I told my fiancée when she started her Salon business to think about the worst that could happen. She could lose some money. Oh well, life goes on, it's not that bad. She's a go-getter! She opened the salon and is doing well. It's probably never as bad as we make it seem. Too much thinking, not enough action, so go out there and get busy!

Chip Away Your Debt

I am not a financial advisor or an expert. However, I was in debt $65,000 and I chipped away at it and made it disappear. Then I managed to get myself in debt years later about $30,000 and also got that down to zero. This was all bad debt, not good debt which I'll explain later. People have different opinions about school loans. I believe if you're focused in on your career then the loans are good because you know what you want. However, if you're drifting and don't have a focus on what you want, I believe in most cases it's a waste of time and money.

I'm going to share with you how I got out of debt. There is no easy way to do it, but there are strategies. There're psychological battles you can win and formulas you can go by. Debt is a weight on our shoulder that beats you down. I remember being so broke that as soon as I finally paid a bill, it was already due again. Can you relate? If so, you should probably pay attention. Then there were bills I couldn't pay. It was a very stressful situation for me. When I started to take responsibility and to have discipline in my spending, things got better. I chipped away, chipped away and chipped away. It was a very long process but well worth it. When you're debt free you can walk with a clear conscience.

So, how did I get so deeply in debt? Well, I was about 21 when I got my first credit card. I still remember buying a double order of wings and a few pitchers of beer. I said, "Wow, it worked!" I went on a spending spree. I got a couple more cards and was having fun. I remember going to the beach and taking money out of the atm over and over; boy was that dumb. My cousin said to me once, "You know you got to pay that back right?" My stepfather tried to teach me some things, but when you're young, it takes time for some things to kick in. I wasn't listening. When you're young, you think you know everything. I was spending foolishly, not a care in the world. I would pay my minimum balance every month...yeah, I know a very uneducated thing to do. If you're only paying your minimum balance, you are probably not in a good situation. I suggest paying your balance in full every month or a big chunk. Believe me; I learned the hard way.

I had doctor bills, credit cards debt, everything you can think of. I was living for the moment and never thought about the future. I was living recklessly. I also had a nice 1998 Pontiac Grand Am when I was around 21. It was a dope car. The problem was I didn't make very good money, and my payments were $99 a month for the first year and $259/mo for the remaining period until it was paid off. Plus, my insurance was expensive. It was around $220 a month. That was way too much for me at that particular time. I had my apartment and all those bills, plus my crazy lifestyle. It didn't add up. I wasn't living right. I missed so many payments, that my car got repossessed, and I owed the balance to the bank after they auctioned it off. On top of all of that was my biggest debt which was school loans, boy did I rack those up.

I was $65,000 in debt and didn't know what to do. My aunt Grace put me onto a company called Consumer Credit. They called my creditors and made deals and consolidated a lot of my debt. Every month I would pay about $350, and it would disperse the money into different debts I owed. Student loans are in a whole different bracket; you have to handle those separately. The problem is not every creditor accepted the offer from Consumer Credit. So, after I paid off the balances, I still owed many different creditors. The process took a few years. It was not fast, and it wasn't fun paying, but I did it. I also started paying on student loans as well. I'm going to be finally done paying on them this year......crazy right. I owed roughly $7,000 on my repo'ed car. I had to pay that separately as well. I was paying a collection agency, and they ended up going out of business. Luckily, I saved all my receipts because a different agency called to collect on the debt. They said that they had no records of me paying anything. If I didn't save those receipts, I would have had to pay it twice or prove in court that I paid it already. Always save your receipts; it saved me from paying $7,000 twice or going to court.

As I said, paying off my debt was a long process that was not fun. However, I gained valuable experience along the way. I learned how important it is to stay on top of your bills and how important your credit is — the creditors that I still owed I called directly and cut deals. You can talk them way down. Let's say you owe $2,500, and you call the agency that owns the debt and say, "Listen I have $1,500 bucks; can I clear my debt with that because it's all I have?" They may or may not accept it, but they might say if you come up with X amount, we will clear it. Each creditor is different, and they do take payments. You may be able to make one initial payment and a few payments after to clear the debt. It's all a game, don't be scared to play.

Remember, "The worst thing someone can say is no." They want their money. The best way to find out what you owe is to buy a full credit report on yourself, and all your debt should come up. Freecreditreport.com or Experian, Credit Karma, and there are many other different sites you can view to find out what you owe and what your score is.

The good thing is you can bounce back pretty quickly. Financial advisors say to have your balances under 30% on your credit cards; it's called credit card utilization. I keep mine a lot lower. I like to use my card then pay it in full when I get the bill. I didn't always have that luxury though. If you're not making a lot of money, then be cautious about how you spend. Don't go nuts like I did when I was younger. Try not to miss or be late on payments, because it negatively affects your credit score. Try not to have too many inquiries. That also affects it. That's when you let people run your credit for certain things like credit cards, cars, houses, etc. Sometimes there's no other way but try and limit it. The age of credit history has an effect also. So, try and keep your cards open so they can age.

Your score ranges from 300-850. Creditors like to see you with a 700 or better if you're trying to buy something big or are looking to get a decent interest rate. Credit Karma is a good app or website to be involved with. It's free, and it tells you your score and what's going on with your accounts. It's not super accurate with the score, but close enough, also if you see something on your credit report that is wrong or not your debt you can dispute it. It's usually as simple as clicking a button and disputing. A lot of times you'll get a favorable outcome.

What I like to do personally is pay off the lower amount of debt first. Let's say you owe an old bill of $250 all the way to thousands. I like knocking out the smallest ones first because you mentally feel the momentum and start killing the debt. Some people like to pay off the highest interest debt first which is smart. The main thing you have to do is come up with extra money. I suggest getting a side job, gig, whatever. Start buying and selling at garage sales or flea markets. Mow some lawns if you're in the hole, you've got to get creative. Come up with extra money so you can pay it off quicker.

It's super important to get started right away. If you're in debt pull your credit report right now, don't waste time. Paying a little is better than nothing, stop making excuses, do it. I was overwhelmed and didn't know what to do, so I simply got started. It took a long time, but I got it done, and to tell you the truth, it's a relief.

There's good debt and bad debt. I would say the majority of the wealthiest people in the world have good debt. Good debt is using leverage to say buy an apartment building. Let's say you put down $50,000 of your own money and borrow $150,000 from the bank. The money borrowed from the bank is good debt. It's getting paid by the tenants from the building and isn't looked at as bad debt. Bad debt is the two different cars you owe money on or the credit cards you ran up. This goes along with assets and liabilities. Assets put money in your pocket while liabilities take money out of your pocket. I got this philosophy from Robert Kiyosaki who wrote all the "Rich Dad Poor Dad" books. I suggest reading them. He says your house is a liability. Bad debt: credit cards, and car payments are bad debt as well as all the materialistic junk we buy.

There's a lot of stuff we buy that is so unnecessary but to each his own. If you're not wealthy, I don't know why your buying $3,000 purses or a $8,000 dollar watch. Be cautious about how you spend your money. When you look at the wealthiest people in the world, they're wearing jeans and a t-shirt. Two years ago, I drove by a 2005 Mercedes Benz all white hard top convertible. It was a dope car. I bought it on the spot. I just sold it a few weeks ago. It was fun, but I didn't need it. I could afford it, but I rarely drove it, so I sold it. It freed up $500 a month between the payment and insurance. Now I'll use that extra money for investing. I've learned the hard way not to be an impulse buyer. I suggest waiting at least one day before making a big purchase – sleep on it. More than likely you'll change your mind. Impulse buying can be financially deadly. If you spend even $20 a day on stupid stuff that's $7,300 a year. That could be your investment money.

You have to really want to make a change for the better. If you want to make power moves, you need good credit. You also have to work on good spending habits. Don't buy things just to buy things. I'm pretty sure we all fall into that trap, but we should be trying to improve every day. Life is good, and we've got to have fun, but try and make intelligent decisions. Write everything down that you owe, plan, and start crossing things off the list. Ask for guidance, ask someone who makes money, not someone who thinks they know everything.

You may be thinking like I did when I was young, *Who cares about my debt and credit?* Well, now more than ever, they look at your credit history when buying houses, cars and everything else. If you want to grow and play in the big leagues, then get it together. Chip away, you'll be glad you got started. Being overwhelmed with debt is a burden you don't want to live with. Get started and get moving. I promise you'll feel like a new man or woman. Hopefully, I helped inspire you to get started. Now Let's Go!

Let It Go:
Stop Living in the Past

I did a lot of wild things in my youth, but the things I did then and the young man I was has no reflection of what I do now or represent the man I am today. Every year I get better, stronger, and smarter. GOD has been molding me, chiseling me, reconstructing me day by day, year by year. I don't live in my past, and I don't do the things I used to. It wouldn't make sense anymore.

When we're young, we think we have got it all figured out. It takes time, experience and education to come into our own. You have to get knocked down a few times, have your heart broken, and have a few bumps and bruises before you're ready for the game of life. We can't walk around in shame or regret. It's important to take responsibility for your actions and face the music. I wouldn't change anything because the road I lived on was bumpy, but I had some of the best times of my life. I traveled the world and met many people with great minds. We have to appreciate the journey and enjoy the process. We can never get our time back so make it count. It's not worth holding onto grudges and hate; we can only make a mark one time here on earth, so let's do it with everything inside us.

"You're not defined by your past; you're prepared by it. You're stronger, more experienced and you have greater confidence"
–Joel Osteen

When I was about 26, it was the time in my life when I knew I had to get it together and stay on the right path. One of my problems was I always beat myself up for the things I did in my past. I was never satisfied with myself and carried a heavy burden constantly. I remember I was at a corner store with my good friend Donnie and we were kicking it and out of nowhere he looked me in the eyes and said, "Matty, you can't keep blaming yourself – you got to let it go." When he said that, everything changed. It was clear. I don't know if you do or don't, but I believe GOD uses people to give us important messages. Sometimes through people, sometimes through signs. It has happened to me many, many times. We have to be conscious of this. Some people shrug it off, but I don't take it lightly. I don't know if Donnie even remembers saying that, but I remember it like it was yesterday. Sometimes we get caught up in our past and all our mistakes. If we continue to go down that road, it begins to become unbearable. However, if you consistently work on yourself, the road becomes much smoother. A prophet prophesied to me. His name is Prophet Copeland. I still have it recorded. He said, "Stop beating yourself up. Stop looking to the past. The Lord doesn't even remember, so why do you? He threw your sins in the ocean of forgetfulness, now let it go and stop bringing it up." This helped me tremendously at the time and even now that I think back on the experience. I think sometimes we're too hard on ourselves. I know I was.

Let it go! If your brother or sister broke your phone or dented your car or didn't pay you back, let it go. I have lent out money to several people who didn't pay me back and guess what, when they come asking again, I simply tell them that I don't lend money on top of money already owed. People will take advantage of you every chance they get, so be careful out there. Watch the angles, don't be ignorant or naive. No matter what, there's always going to be reasons for us to be mad at sibling's, friends, wives, husbands, whatever. It's just not worth carrying the weight.

I believe that we cannot be truly blessed if we hold on to grudges. How can we reach our full potential if we're walking around mad and full of anger? If you learn to let go you can focus on yourself better and the people you love and the things that need to get done. I choose not to stay mad at people. It may take me 2 seconds, or maybe a day or two to get over it, but in that time, I'm analyzing the situation, looking at all angles, and trying to understand everything that occurred. I know I'm not perfect, I've messed up plenty of times and I'll mess up again. However, I have a very strong character; I know when to apologize when I did something wrong. It's not hard for me to apologize. See GOD gave me a good judge of character and a moral compass. When I'm off, I know I'm off.

If I offend someone or say something wrong, I know it right away, or soon after. Try and fix the problem and come up with a solution. Some people refuse to apologize, and those are usually the people walking around angry with themselves. That can cause stomach problems and health problems, along with misery. I know how to accept fault, and when the situation calls for it, I handle my business. There will be times when people don't accept your apology, and it is what it is. Don't chase them, you said what you felt was necessary and tried, that's all you can do.

Sometimes, we make a bigger deal of things than what they really are. Like the guy at Burger King who puts onions on your burger and you said no onions, so you go in there and start screaming. Sorry to tell you, but you're not representing yourself very well. You could have simply taken them off and threw them away or go back in and politely say, excuse me I asked for no onions, can I have a new burger. That's all. Yeah sometimes it's frustrating, but how many mistakes have you made? I know I've made a ton. Every single day in our lives, we have a split second to make a choice when a conflict occurs. Someone cuts you off in traffic, so you speed up and flip them off and scream at the other driver. In this day and age who knows what the result could be? Take a deep breath, put on some Bob Marley, relax and let it go. 99.9 % of the time it's not worth getting mad. Believe me, I'm no saint, I've fallen in the trap when I'm driving so, I know it can be hard. That's why I stay prayed up 24/7. Life isn't easy, I know, but we all have the choice of how to react or respond. I tell people when they're mad don't send that text back right away or don't call back right away, give it a few minutes, breathe, think about it, sleep on it. A lot of the time our reactions are much harsher then we want them to be. Life is too good and too short to be angry all the time. Enjoy it, let go of the anger and chaos... be easy out there my people.

Sometimes we create or imagine things that aren't even there or get upset at something that didn't even happen. I know there's a lot of people out there that feel me, don't lie, you've done it before. You'll be driving and thinking of a scenario that didn't happen, and you start working yourself up. Ha-ha, we probably all have done it at some point in our life. What's important is we grow out of it and strive for greater, stronger, more positive thoughts.

There's a story about a woman who talked about her family members all getting cancer. She talked about it to her family, friends, and strangers. She would say I know I'm going to get cancer; my mom had it, my sisters, so on and so on. Well, she got cancer and died from it. Who's to say if she kept a positive attitude and said I'm healthy and strong her whole life that it wouldn't have happened to her? Some people don't believe words and thoughts have power. However, I'm here to tell you through my personal experiences they do. It's good to be prepared, but why worry about something that isn't there or doesn't exist? You're wasting precious time on nothing.

When I'm in the wrong, I like to make it right, or at least try. I'm far from perfect, but at this point in my life, I try my best to do the right thing. We should all strive to work things out for the best. I'm someone who forgives very easily if the person apologizing is sincere. Why hold a grudge if they apologize, and if they don't apologize, I let it go anyway! Some situations call for different outcomes. It may not be pretty but find a way to try and make it work. There have been a lot of shady things thrown my way. People have accused me of things and tried to assassinate my character, but in the end, I rose to greatness through the grace of GOD. I pushed forward and never gave up. If you're someone who is holding on to grudges and pain, I suggest you find a way to let, go. Dig deep! I understand and feel you, but to reach the mountaintop, we have to let go of the baggage. It's a relief when you say to yourself, *You know what, I'm releasing that thing that's on my back, and I forgive that person, and I'm moving on.* Don't let someone else contradict your movements and happiness. Life is to good, and life is too short to stay angry.

It gets deep, because someone reading this may have been taken advantage of, going through depression, struggling with addictions, a bad separation, someone may have taken a loved one's life away from you, or you lost someone you loved. I've lost family, friends, close people in my life, and I know everything I mentioned can be unbearably hard to deal with. I'm writing this for you, for us. There is no absolute answer that I can personally give, but I can say be selfish for once and think about yourself. It's not fair for you to be going through so much pain, but don't give the situation or person strength. I went through things that were hard to let go, but I did. You'll still think about it from time to time, but the pain weakens, and you become stronger. Push, love, believe, have faith, know that you can get through.

Find something you love and be around that love. Running, biking, dogs, cats, singing, drawing, writing, planting, sewing, boxing, whatever it may be and persist in love. Honestly, I wrote this book because I wanted to try and help people. So, if I can help you to believe in yourself more and more every day, then that would make me feel grateful. I know I have a lot more to do before I leave this planet, but this book is a good start. I appreciate you for taking the time to read this; it means a lot to me. When it comes down to it, when we strip away all the extra junk, it's about us, us as people. We have to treat each other better, stop being so judgmental and respect each other. If we all contribute to helping someone a couple of times a day, we would all be going in the right direction. I have nothing but love for you.

This is the End

D ig deep, find a way, be you! Love yourself and don't beat yourself up too much. Enjoy yourself. There is only one you, you're special and unique. Don't worry so much about other people's opinions. If you have people in your life that help you get to the next level and they're honest with you, then cherish them, love them and have their back to the end. There are not too many people who you can count on, so when you find them treat them well.

Set goals, stay active and keep moving forward. Raise your standards, don't accept anyone who mistreats you. If you're not happy in your current situation, then make a move, make a change. Train your mind to be fearless. Trust in GOD, and everything else will follow. Every year you should be getting better. It's a process, but a fine wine takes time. Chisel the negativity off yourself and step into greatness. Every year eat better, exercise more, save more to invest, be smarter with your money and spending habits and if you're in debt start chipping away at it immediately. Make someone smile, give compliments, and enjoy life. Invest in yourself, read more, learn more, listen more, teach more, help more, love more. Focus on what's in front of you, stay in your lane and have a laser focus on the things you set out to achieve.

Don't be scared to get started at whatever it is you want to do. Go for it! Stop procrastinating and put your dreams in action. Travel and explore. My mom taught me to smell the roses, look around and be grateful for what you have. Life is good, don't let it pass you by. Remember when our back is against the wall, that's when we can truly test ourselves and become extremely creative. It's good to be in difficult situations, because that's how we grow and get better. Don't look at your problems as a bad thing, look at them as building blocks to your success. The more practice you have in tight situations, the better of a leader you'll become.

Life is very challenging, and you're guaranteed to have rough days, it's how we respond to the challenges that matter most. When you get a curve ball thrown at you, you have to stay grounded and keep your eyes on the ball. Swing for the fences! Be ready for anything. Be mentally prepared for the game of life. When you leave the house in the morning, talk to yourself and have a bulletproof mentality for all negativity. Have a shield around you that deflects all negative vibes. Stay positive and mentally ready for whatever. Be careful who you hang with, put yourself in good situations and a good atmosphere. If you feel a strange vibe in your gut, be on alert. Follow your instincts; it's very important.

Gratitude and attitude are essential to our well-being. Try not to take anything for granted; you never know what can happen. Every morning I wake up, I thank GOD for another day. The way you come across to people comes from the energy you're giving out, and most likely it's going to come back. If you're holding on to hate or grudges, let it go. It's not worth carrying that junk in your belly. It's healthier for the mind, body, and soul to have a clear conscience and feel a sense of freedom. Trust me; you'll feel better.

I'm very blessed and thankful that you took the time out of your busy life and schedule to read this book. I appreciate you to the fullest. Thank you! I truly pray and hope that I had some positive impact on your life and I hope that I touched you in some positive way. I came from a humble beginning but have always had love in my life, and for that, I am blessed. I'm grateful that I have a good mother who raised me right which I know wasn't easy. I have an amazing family, my fiancée and kids that I love dearly, and I'm blessed to be where I am. I've had my ups and downs, my roadblocks, obstacles, and challenges but I never stop fighting, I never stop believing and I'll keep pushing forward until the day I'm gone. I feel like I haven't even scratched the surface yet. I know there's so much more to come.

Believe in yourself and have confidence in your abilities, don't ever give up. Feed your mind good things, and positivity will be attracted to you. The things you stay focused on will gravitate towards you. Remember we're not perfect and we will never be perfect. There's going to be times we make the wrong decision, and that's ok, it's part of life. There's going to be times when we say something for which we may have to apologize later. It is what it is. What's important is we try our best and recognize these situations and confront them.

I hope everyone who reads this book enjoyed it. Send me a message on Facebook or Instagram under Matty Guariglia, or visit my website www.mattyguariglia.com and tell me your thoughts and opinions; it would mean a lot. If you enjoyed it and thought it could help someone else, please share it with them. I appreciate it. GOD bless! I hope you reach greatness and reach a life of abundance. Be easy and stay blessed — one love.

About the Author

Matthew Guariglia was raised by a hard working single mother. She was a strong Italian woman. Although they did not have much money, they had a lot of love and a good foundation. Matt's mom cut hair out of the kitchen to make ends meet, which Matt believes had something to do with his entrepreneurial spirit and natural ability to make things happen.

In his 20's, Matt was on his own. He managed to get an Associate Degree in Social Science, but found himself $65,000 in debt along the way. He was dead broke, taking cold showers and at one point, he had no heat for an entire year. His car got repossessed and his environment was holding him back. He knew it was time for a change.

Matt prayed to GOD for an opportunity and shortly thereafter an opportunity presented itself. Matt got a job in the roofing field and climbed his way up from laborer to roofer, and eventually started his own business with a partner. To build their business, they knocked on doors two years straight with not a single day off. This paid off for Matt. He has a fire inside that burns deep. He has never looked back or wondered, "What if it doesn't work?" He knew it would. Whatever you want in life you have to go "all in" and do it with fire.

Matt Guariglia can be reached at http:// mattyguariglia.com.

52718461R00067

Made in the USA
Columbia, SC
11 March 2019